DOSH

Wren & Rook
An imprint of
Hachette Children's Group
Part of Hodder & Stoughton
Carmelite House
50 Victoria Embankment
London EC4Y 0DZ

A Hachette UK Company
www.hachette.co.uk
www.hachettechildrens.co.uk

Publishing Director: Debbie Foy
Commissioning Editor: Laura Horsley
Art Director: Laura Hambleton
Production Controller: Kelly Llewellyn
Designed by Kathryn Slack

Printed in China

DOSH

BY RASHMI SIRDESHPANDE

ILLUSTRATED BY ADAM HAYES

wren
&rook

'FOR MY FATHER; THE MOST GENEROUS PERSON I KNOW' –
R. S.

CONTENTS

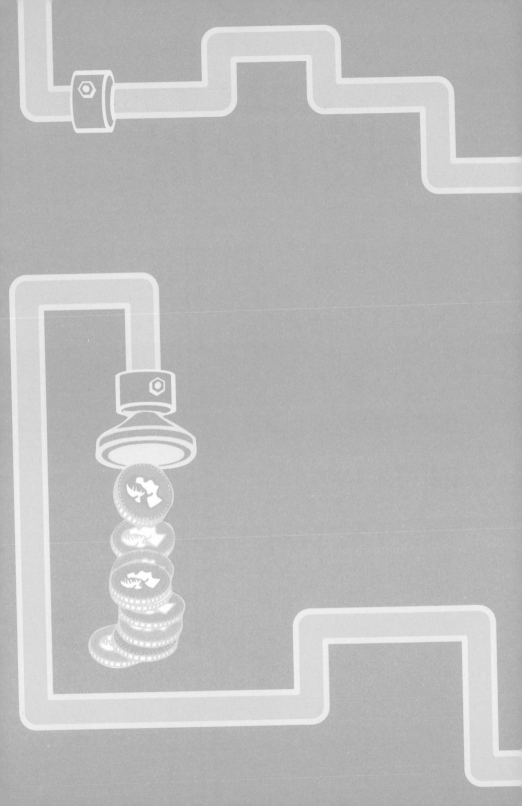

It's got **LOTS** of names and comes in different shapes and forms, but **MONEY** has been used all over the world for thousands of years to buy things, build things and to change lives. What do you think of when you think of money? Piles of gold stacked up high? *Finally* buying that guitar you've been saving up for? Or living a life of luxury like a rich celebrity? Money can make all of this happen, but first you need to understand how it works, how to get it and what to do with it when you do. Once you know *that*, you can start to have some fun. Today, that might mean getting your hands on that guitar. Years from now, it could mean living the kind of life you've always dreamed of. That may seem **SO** far away, but developing good money habits (and knowing what to do when things aren't going too well) will help set you off on the right track. That's where this book comes in.

BUT WAIT. WHAT IS MONEY?

Money has changed quite a bit over time – from metal coins to paper to plastic to cards held in a digital wallet on a mobile phone. But what it *does* hasn't changed:

1 **IT'S A MEDIUM OF EXCHANGE** Now you might be wondering what on earth that means, but it's just a fancy way of saying we use money to buy and sell stuff. Simple.

2 **IT'S A STORE OF VALUE** This just means we don't have to spend it all right away. We can sit on it and use it later or save it up if we need more of it. Saving up for a flight into space? No probs. (Tickets *are* actually on sale now, by the way, just very pricey.)

3 **IT'S A UNIT OF ACCOUNT** We can count it so we know how much we've got – *very* handy! – and we can use it to put a price on things and to compare prices too.

Money sometimes gets a bad reputation. But money itself isn't good or bad – it's what you do with it that matters. And if you learn how to use it effectively, it can be empowering and a real force for good in the world. At a very basic level, the fact is we

need it. Money is the thing that gives you a house to sleep in, delicious food to eat and clothes to wear. It can give you an education and it can take care of your health. Money can help someone set up a business and support their family. It can rebuild whole cities after a disaster. **YEP, MONEY CAN BE GREAT.**

But money *can* sometimes be bad. It can be used to fund corrupt things. It can stress us out. Some people worry that they don't have enough. Some people even fight over money. Some people think money will make them happy and *more* money will make them even happier. But you can be rich and unhappy, and you can have next to nothing and be extremely happy! You can keep wanting more and more (even billionaires have an island somewhere they can't quite afford!) but at some point, it's worth stopping to be grateful for what you've got. Besides, once you've got the basics covered, the best things in life really are free – like hanging out and laughing with good friends.

So we need to figure out how to use money for good (and never **EVER** for bad), to have enough of it to get by, and to be in control of it rather than letting it eat us up!

MONEY IS A TOOL

When we say we want money, what we *really* mean is that we want all the things that having money lets us *do* and *experience* and the kind of life it lets us live. Staring at stacks of money all day like a baddie in a movie isn't too much fun, but you can use that money to go out and travel the world. And though you can't *eat* money, you can use it to buy a scrummy chocolate cake. Or a warm meal for someone who needs one. Maybe we don't need stacks of money anyway — maybe what we're after is having enough to get by, to live a decent and comfortable. life. It's those end-goals we want, not the paper or coins we use to get them.

Now, unless you've got a magic lamp somewhere, you'll have a limited amount of money and you'll need to decide what to do with it. That means *prioritising* and making *choices.*

PRIORITISING = LISTING THINGS

FROM SUPER-IMPORTANT

TO

MEH. NOT REALLY THAT IMPORTANT AFTER ALL.

The bad news is that these are two things humans can be *terrible* at.

The good news is that it's all fixable. If we do a bit of thinking instead of rushing into things, we *can* make good choices.

BACK UP. What choices? Well, every single time you get hold of some money, you can choose to:

These choices are all part of **managing your money**.

Managing your money. Be honest. Does that sound boring? For many, many grown-ups, it isn't just boring, it's downright scary.

And **BORING + SCARY = A DANGEROUS COMBINATION.** You see, for the longest time, this wasn't something that was taught at home or at school. You just grew up and – **BOOM!** – you were expected to get on with it.

No one taught me this stuff either. I had no idea. And it all sounded so *amazingly* dull that I never bothered to look it up. Until I grew up and had all these bills and all these dreams and … well … I had to figure it all out. **OK,** I knew a *few* things about money – I knew that growing up we didn't have much of it and my parents worked really hard to make more. I saw that my parents used the money they did have to do good things, to help people out, and because of them I learned that money was something you *respect* (and something you look after). At the same time, I saw people around me who really struggled with it – people who couldn't pay their bills or afford the things and the kind of life they had hoped for, even though they were often doing the best they could.

Lots of people go through financial difficulties and it's nothing to be ashamed of. The truth is that there are often lots of things outside of our control and people's fortunes can change dramatically. But by knowing how best to manage your money, you can be as prepared as possible and hopefully avoid getting into those situations. And if you *do* end up in trouble, you can come up with a plan to deal with it. Think of this book as your ultimate money handbook. Your portable partner in crime. Your cheat sheet to help you decide what to do with your **DOSH**, how to look after it and what to do if things get tricky.

Here's what we're going to do.

First, we'll look at **WHAT MONEY IS**, how it's changed over the years, and where it might be headed.

Then, we'll talk about **HOW TO EARN IT**. We'll think about skills you can work on *today* to supercharge your earning power *tomorrow*. We'll think about jobs – sure – but also how to set up your own business (and **PSSST**, I've got some ideas that you can get started with right away!).

Next, the *exciting* bit: **HOW TO SPEND YOUR MONEY**. We know all about that. Or do we? Spending like a pro means knowing where to splash your cash and how to avoid being swayed by all that tricksy advertising. We'll talk about choices and thinking ahead and we'll learn how to draw up a **budget** (a clever word for a good old-fashioned **PLAN**).

Then, we'll get to the not-so-fun but *very* important question of **HOW TO SAVE**. Get this right and get in early and some years from now, you could be laughing all the way to the bank. Speaking of banks, we'll talk about those too. It's good to know how they work.

After that, it's the biggie: **HOW TO GROW YOUR MONEY**. They say money doesn't grow on trees and that's true – it doesn't. But it does *grow*. We'll look at *how* to grow it. Saving is just one way to do it.

THIS IS A MONEY TREE.
One of many varieties of money tree. What do you notice? That's right. No money. They're lovely plants, though, and many people believe they bring good luck.

Last but by no means least is **HOW TO GIVE MONEY**. There are lots of ways to do this. The more money you earn, save and grow, the more *wealth* you'll create (we'll get to that on page 113!) and the more money you can *give* to the causes that you care about. And even when you haven't got much money to give, there's something you *do* have and that's *time*. You can give *that* generously too.

GOT ALL THAT? GOOD.
LET'S GET STARTED.

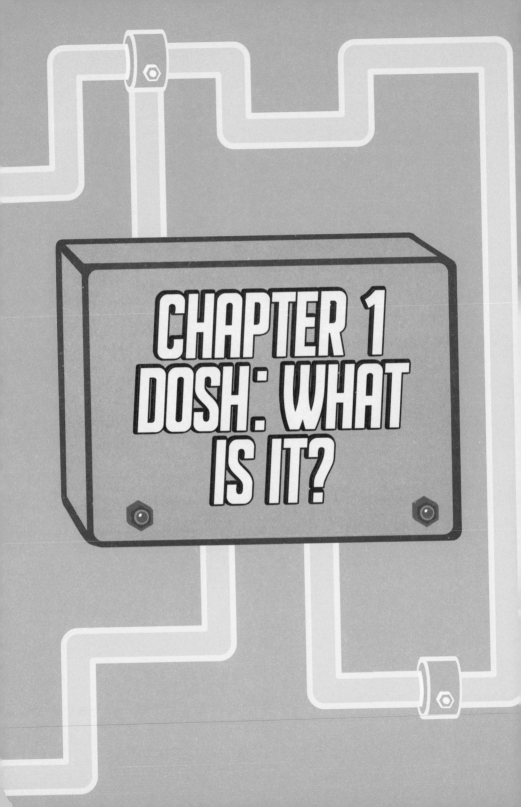

CHAPTER 1
DOSH: WHAT IS IT?

Today, when you hear the word 'money', you might think of notes and coins. Maybe a credit card or an app. But *way* back, things were different. If you needed something, you had to swap something else for it. This system was called BARTERING. Imagine that! If you wanted a bit of food, you had to give up something in order to get it. *What* you gave up depended on what the other person wanted. And how much you gave up depended on how *badly* they wanted it.

Bartering isn't easy. You can't just prance into a sweltering desert and offer someone a woolly jumper in exchange for an ice cream. They just won't want it (unless it's the kind of desert that gets really cold at night). But if you offer a bottle of water in exchange for that ice cream, you might just have a deal …

Bartering was first recorded in Egypt around 9000 BCE. Back then, people bartered with all kinds of things from cows and sheep to grains and vegetables. Over time, trade routes developed between cities and merchants started trading things like weapons, precious stones, spices and salt.

This kind of travel made shopping *much* more exciting but it also created some problems.

CATTLE CAN BE TRICKY TO TRANSPORT.

GRAINS AND VEGETABLES CAN ROT.

AND CROPS ARE A BIT OF A PROBLEM ANYWAY.

What if you want to store everything so you can trade *later*?
How long are those veggies going to last? Worse still, what
happens if you have a bad harvest? And what happens if the
person you need to trade with doesn't like any of your stuff?

Bartering didn't stop when coins and notes were introduced. It just became much more organised. Around 130 CE, the Han Dynasty in China opened up the Silk Road, a series of trade routes between the Far East and Europe. Merchants travelled in groups called caravans, trading things like tea and silks from China, fine cotton and spices from India, dates and pistachio nuts from the Middle East, and glass, gold, and silver from the Mediterranean.

In fact, people still barter today. Some companies barter, swapping products and services instead of paying cash. Ever swapped anything like a toy, book, snack or clothing with a friend or a sibling? If so, you've been bartering too!

Wouldn't it be so much better if you could use *something* else to buy and sell things? Something more portable and long-lasting? Something everyone could accept? Well, this is where coins and notes would come in handy …

MONEY: A SUPER QUICK HISTORY

CLINK CLANK COINS - 2000 BCE

Silver rings or **coils** are used as money in Mesopotamia (now Iraq and Syria), long before the first coins are made. Their value is measured by weight in 'shekels'. One month's labour is worth about 1 shekel. Under the laws of the city of Eshnunna, if you slap someone's cheek you'll be fined 10 shekels. Biting someone's nose will cost you 60! **GULP**.

SHE SELLS SEA SHELLS - 1200 BCE

In parts of India and China, people use **cowrie shells** as money. They're much easier than hauling cattle or cartloads of grain around. They're small and sturdy and, because of their shape and texture, they're *really* hard to fake.

Around 2,000 years later, traders will introduce these shells to West Africa. Between 1700 and 1790, the Dutch and the British will transport around 10 billion cowrie shells from the Indian Ocean to West Africa in exchange for millions of slaves. This is when money isn't a good thing. Some people do terrible, terrible things because they're greedy for more.

MINTED KINGS - 600 BCE

Some of the world's first **coins** are **minted** in Lydia (now Turkey) during this time. Made of electrum, a mix of gold and silver, they have a roaring lion on them and they have the backing of the king, who has guaranteed their quality. The Lydian kings, by the way, are famous for their wealth. Ever heard of the term 'rich as Croesus' (*sounds like 'creases'*)? Croesus was the last Lydian king and he was made of money.

KING MIDAS AND HIS GOLDEN TOUCH

The Pactolus River was an important source of electrum in Lydia. According to Ancient Greek legend, it's all because the King Midas rinsed his hands in the river to wash away his Golden Touch! Midas's story is one of greed. The cheeky god Dionysus granted the King's wish that everything he touched would turn to gold. It made him super-rich, all right, but at quite a cost. His family, food and drink all turned to solid gold. Midas was in pieces. He begged Dionysus for a cure and was told to bathe in the river where he could wash his golden touch away.

Suddenly, coins are all the rage. Everyone wants to use them. They catch on in places like Athens and Rome. Before this, Athenians were using *iron nails* as money – **MASSIVE** health and safety fail!

FROM SPADES TO COINS - 221 BCE

The first Emperor of China, Qin Shi Huangdi, unifies the country and introduces a universal **bronze coin**, banning all other local coins. Before this, people often used mini bronze replicas of spades and knives as money. Much more portable than actual spades and knives but still very spiky! You wouldn't want to pop *those* in your pocket and forget about them! This new coin is nice and round and it has a square hole in the middle so it can be carried on a string. Pretty and practical? **VERY**. But also, in ancient China, it was believed that the Earth was square and the heavens were domed, so this little coin is a symbol of harmony between Heaven and Earth. Nice, eh?

PAPER MONEY!

FLYING MONEY - 806 CE

Chinese merchants make *paper* money because coins are too bulky for big purchases and because there just aren't enough to go around. They call this *fei chien* or 'flying money' because it's so light that it can fly away in the breeze. It's basically an 'I-owe-you' (an IOU) – a promise that this paper can be swapped for coins later on. So merchants trade using paper money then pop back home to exchange it. That's how it all begins, but within a few hundred years, the Chinese government starts issuing official paper currency too.

MAKING GOLD FROM NOTHING - 1275—92

Venetian explorer Marco Polo discovers paper money on his travels to China. It's like alchemy — making gold from *nothing*. Turning paper, of all things, into actual *money*. It's light and it's cheap and it's basically wonderful. Marco Polo brings the idea back to Europe, all excited. But the Europeans aren't too sure. It'll be another 300 years before they start to use paper notes.

FAKE MONEY

This paper money from China is a type of **fiat money**. That just means that the paper used for notes (and the metal used in coins) isn't actually worth much. The value comes from the fact that the government says, 'Hey, this is money' (in fact, in Latin, *fiat* means 'let it be done'). As long as people trust the government and its laws, this is fine. But if people lose trust, the value of that money goes **RIGHT** down.

The money we use today is also fiat money. And because the materials used to print fiat money aren't precious, *some* sneaky people try to print fake money and make counterfeit coins. But this isn't easy to do. Coins can have detailed patterns and ridged edges to make them hard to forge. Notes also have clever security features like watermarks and holograms, and you can test them using UV-light or detector pens, which will only mark fake notes!

I OWE YOU - 1661

Banknotes are printed in Sweden - the first in Europe. *Finally.* (The first paper money in what we now call the USA will be printed in 1690 by the Massachusetts Bay Colony). Copper coins are heavy and a hassle to carry around, so Sweden's first ever bank, Stockholms Banco, issues notes that can be used as an IOU. Thing is, it issues more IOUs than the coins it's got (it's hoping that not everyone will want to withdraw their cash from the bank at the same time!).

It's working well, so the bank prints more notes. And *more*. And *more*. With lots of notes around, they're not worth as much any longer. So people rush to the bank to change their IOUs into good old copper coins. But it doesn't have enough! **UH-OH.** So the bank goes bust and lots of people lose their savings. It's awful. And, as we'll see on page 28, it's not the last time something like this will happen ...

INVISIBLE MONEY

MAGIC MONEY - 1871

Western Union arranges the world's first **electronic money transfer.** They call it 'wiring' money. This is a **BIG** deal. Money moving from one place to another without actually *physically moving* from one place to another? **MAGIC!**

1929–39

THE GREAT DEPRESSION

Do you know that scene in *Mary Poppins* where a little boy, Michael Banks, wants his money back from the bank and people overhear and panic because they think that everyone wants their money out? And then, because of that, everyone *does* want their money out and, just like in Sweden in the 1600s, the bank doesn't have enough cash to go around and it's all a great big disaster? Well, that's exactly what happened in 1929 and 1930 in the USA when something called the stock market crashed (we'll talk about the stock market on page 122).

There were rumours going around that the banks didn't have enough money, so people panicked and tried to take their money out of their accounts. And because *everyone* was asking for their money and the bank just didn't have enough, the banks *did* go bust. Thousands of them. And many people lost ALL their savings. This led to the Great Depression, a long, terrible period of people losing their jobs and even their homes.

1950
'I FORGOT MY WALLET!'

The first **credit card** is created in 1950. Frank McNamara comes up with the idea when he forgets his wallet and can't pay for his dinner at a New York City restaurant (his wife has to come and bail him out!). He's *totally* embarrassed and he decides he's not going to let *that* happen again. So he creates the Diners Club Card. It's just a small cardboard thing but the idea takes off. People use it to pay for stuff and they just get charged at the end of the month. Within five years, the card is accepted in countries across the world and by 1959 the Diners Club has **ONE MILLION** members!

By the 1960s and 1970s credit cards are everywhere! They make spending really easy as you don't have to carry cash around any more. Unlike the early credit cards (like the Diners Club Card) where you had to pay the credit card company in full each month, *now* people can spend money *they don't even have* and pay fees (interest) to the credit card company.

THIS is where things started to get dangerous. Cards are so easy and quick to use and if you're not very good at remembering how much money you have and how much you're spending, you can get into a **LOT** of trouble. More on that in the next chapter.

ONLINE MONEY- 1990S

Internet banking takes off. It had started in the 1980s but it's finally picking up and it changes everything. Now people can spend and transfer money with the click of a button. And they can check their accounts online to see how much they've spent and how much they have left. Today, most of the money in the world is electronic. It isn't physically sitting in a bank somewhere. It's a line of code on the bank's computer with your name on it!

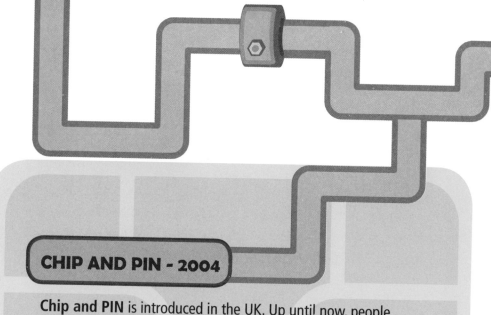

CHIP AND PIN - 2004

Chip and PIN is introduced in the UK. Up until now, people using bank cards have had to swipe their card using a card machine and sign a receipt every time they buy something. But magnetic swipe cards can be cloned and signatures are so easy to fake! Chip and PIN cards are much more secure. And when the card is put into a PIN machine, the cardholder needs to enter their secret four-digit PIN (Personal Identification Number) in order to use it. It makes life much harder for criminals as long as people don't go for obvious four-digit combos like 1234, birthday years, or something like 2580 — yep, it looks random, but it's actually just all the numbers in the middle of the keypad from top to bottom … *AVOID!*

£ 📱 😄 - 2007

Mobile banking becomes really popular with more and more banks building fancy apps for smartphones. But it's not just about swishy smartphones! In Kenya, thanks to a service called M-Pesa, even the simplest phones can now be used to send money using text messages!

Contactless payments are rolled out in a big way in the UK. Splashing your cash is now as easy as tapping a contactless bank card against a PIN machine (and soon, holding a smartphone near a PIN machine). **EASY-PEASY**. *Too* easy. Tapping doesn't even *feel* like spending. Luckily, payments are usually capped to help stop people spending **ALL** their money without realising!

Contactless payments have a slower start in other countries but over the next 12 years, they become very popular in places like Australia, Canada, Singapore and Sweden (which is set to become a fully cashless society by 2030)!

CRYPTOPCURRENCY - 2009

BITCOIN IS CREATED. IT'S THE FIRST **CRYPTOCURRENCY** OR **DIGITAL CURRENCY**. IT WORKS JUST LIKE MONEY BUT IT'S COMPLETELY **VIRTUAL** (NO NOTES AND COINS ANYWHERE). MORE ON THIS ON PAGE 36!

FOREIGN CURRENCIES

Now one thing that can get a little confusing is when we're on holiday and suddenly the money seems completely different – we might see dollars (and different types of dollars!), pounds, euros, yen, rupees, pesos and more and we spend AGES busting our brains trying to calculate what they actually mean. This is because each country typically has its own type of money – we call this a **currency.** For instance, most of the examples I use in this book will be in UK pounds – a currency sometimes confusingly called 'sterling'! – because I'm British, but if you're reading this in another country, you can convert pounds to dollars or euros or whatever currency you use every day. People will buy and sell things using local currency and if you're travelling to another country, you'll need some too. You can get this from a bank or exchange bureau and how much you can get for your money depends on the exchange rate. This tells you what one currency is worth in relation to the other.

For example, if you live in APPLE LAND where the currency is apples and you're off to PEAR LAND where the currency is pears, you'd look at the exchange rate to see how many pears you can get for your apples.

EXCHANGE BUREAU

1 APPLE =
2 PEARS

Right, that's two pears for every apple. So if you need six pears for your trip, you'll need to trade three apples. That's if you're converting your currency *today*. Exchange rates change all the time. Lots of things can affect how valuable a currency is, including how much people trust the government. If the world loses faith in the government of Apple Land, the value of apples will go down and you'll need to spend a lot more of them to get your pears!

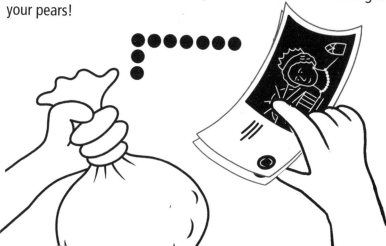

CRYPTOCURRENCIES

BITCOIN • WHAT'S ALL THE FUSS ABOUT AND WHAT IS IT ANYWAY?

Cryptocurrencies like Bitcoin are very new and *very* exciting. Trouble is, they're so new and exciting that people are still trying to wrap their brains around them. But we're going to give it a shot, **OK**?

Right. So Bitcoin only exists in computer code – there aren't any physical coins and notes that you can put in your pocket. It's a bit like virtual money or tokens you collect in a video game, except that it's *real* and you can send it to someone else or use it to buy real things wherever it's accepted (and it isn't accepted everywhere!).

There are two main things you need to know about it:

1 IT CUTS OUT BANKS AND GOVERNMENTS

Why? Because not everyone trusts them! Remember the Great Depression? That was bad. And banks had a big role to play in the global financial crisis of 2008 too (more on that on page 130). With most currencies, the government controls the supply of money. And every time you send or spend it, your payments go through a bank. With Bitcoin, everything happens between *individuals*.

2 IT'S SUPER-SECURE

Bitcoin is an **encrypted** computer file. 'Encrypted' just means it's protected by secret codes that make it very difficult to hack. So your money (and your identity) should be kept safe!

Bitcoin was created by a **MYSTEEEERIOUS** person or group of people called **Satoshi Nakamoto**. We still don't know who they are.

Every time Bitcoin is sent or spent, that **transaction** is recorded in an electronic public record called the **blockchain.** It covers every Bitcoin transaction in the history of the world and anyone can see it, but everyone's identity is kept secret.

Now, before a transaction is added to the blockchain, it has to be checked by **bitcoin miners** all over the world. These miners don't have hard hats or pickaxes – just *very* powerful computers that solve some very tricky maths puzzles. If they're the first to solve the puzzle, they're rewarded with some Bitcoin. This is how Bitcoin is made. It's *mined.*

$$10 - 3 \div \frac{2}{5} + 6 = Z^3$$

$$-\frac{1}{2} Z + X^4 - ie + 10^5$$

$$\sqrt{1 - V^2} \quad X^3 + Y^3 + Z^2$$

$$\frac{X^3}{693.52} \quad F = \frac{ZX}{4}$$

$$(a, b)$$

Mining for Bitcoin is like mining for **GOLD**. It's jolly hard work and there's a limited supply of Bitcoin out there – just 21 million in total!

BUT THERE'S A DARK SIDE TO BITCOIN TOO ...

There's a big environmental downside – this mining hardware uses up a **LOT** of electricity. Some people believe it uses up as much electricity as a small country! The other issue is that because everyone's identity is kept secret in the blockchain, it's the perfect currency for the **BADDEST BADDIES** who naturally want to be anonymous. But the police can use some clever maths of their own to trace anyone who is up to no good!

WHERE CAN YOU GET HOLD OF BITCOIN?

Like any other currency, Bitcoin can be bought at the going exchange rate, except this has to be done at a cryptocurrency exchange like Coinbase and you'll need a Bitcoin wallet in order to do it. If you live in Apple Land, the exchange rate will tell you how many apples you need to cough up for a piece of Bitcoin. Yes, that's right – you don't have to buy a whole Bitcoin (that could be quite costly!). You can just buy a fraction.

THE FUTURE OF MONEY

There are *lots of* cryptocurrencies out there and the truth is that even the grown-ups are still figuring it all out. Don't believe that? Ask the one nearest to you! One thing's for sure – every single time a new form of money has caught on in the world, it's changed the way we live our lives. Cryptocurrencies are still fairly new and we haven't yet seen all the exciting things they might open up. Or the risks and dangers they may have in store. Let's just say it's something to keep an eye on …

DOSH IN A NUTSHELL

* **IN THE EARLY DAYS,** way before notes and coins, people bartered things like cattle and grain But cattle is tough to transport and grains can rot. And what do you do if no one wants the stuff you have to offer?

* **SO, COINS WERE DEVELOPED** – they took different forms around the world from cowrie shells to mini replicas of knives but they were all portable, long-lasting and something everyone could accept.

* **THE FIRST COINS** (as we'd recognise them today!) were minted in Lydia around 600 BCE.

✳ **PAPER MONEY** was first used by merchants in China around 806 CE.

✳ **MUCH LATER, IN THE 1900s,** there was a rise in *invisible money* with credit cards, internet banking and super-fast contactless payments making sending and *spending* money so much easier.

✳ **IN 2009, THE WORLD'S FIRST CRYPTOCURRENCY** was created – Bitcoin. It's completely virtual and it's designed to be very secure.

✳ **EVERY TIME A NEW FORM OF MONEY** has been invented, it's changed the way we do things. Maybe, in time, cryptocurrency will too. And who knows what kind of money we might be using in the future!

SO. NOW YOU KNOW WHAT DOSH IS, HOW IT HAS CHANGED AND WHERE IT MIGHT BE HEADED, IT'S TIME TO THINK ABOUT MAKING SOME OF IT. OR LOTS OF IT, EVEN.

CHAPTER 2
HOW TO
EARN IT

WHERE DOES MONEY COME FROM?

Money isn't just going to magically appear out of nowhere (unless you really have found that genie … and if you *have*, what are you doing with this book?!). If you want money, what you need to do is to **EARN** it. **WORK FOR IT.** This means trading your time, energy and skills for money. But before we get to that …

WHY DO YOU WANT THAT MONEY, ANYWAY?

Think about what really matters to you.

WHAT KIND OF LIFE WOULD YOU LIKE TO HAVE?

WHAT KIND OF PERSON DO YOU WANT TO BE?

A TOP FOOTBALLER?

SOMEONE REALLY ARTISTIC?

SOMEONE WITH ALL THE LATEST GADGETS?

SOMEONE WHO GIVES LOADS TO CHARITY?

WHAT ABOUT RIGHT NOW?

ANY IDEAS FOR REDECORATING YOUR BEDROOM?

GOT YOUR EYE ON A NEW BIKE?

Now you can take all that good stuff and keep it in your head, scribble it down somewhere safe, or put together a vision board.

HOLIDAY

CAR

HOUSE

MUSIC

MY VISION BOARD.

To create a vision board, write, draw and doodle all the things you'd like to save up for. Cut things you like out of magazines and chuck in some goals and words that inspire you. **YES, IT'S CHEESY,** but a bit of cheese never hurt anyone. When your vision board is ready, take a good look at it. You might find some of the stuff on there doesn't cost a penny and that's great! Put your vision board up somewhere where you'll see it lots. It's a reminder of where you want to get to and what's important to you.

Now you should have more of an idea of *why* you want money, let's look at how you go about earning it …

MONEY TODAY

Maybe you already receive an allowance or pocket money that goes into a money bank. Maybe you have an opportunity to do some chores around the house or to earn an allowance some other way. Or maybe you don't! Some people can't afford to give out allowances or pocket money or would rather not, and that's totally their decision (my parents couldn't!). So be nice and be *patient*.

But if earning an allowance is an option, there are two things to ask yourself:

1 WHAT DO PEOPLE NEED?

2 WHAT DO I HAVE TO GIVE?

In business, when someone's needs or *wants* match up with something you have to give, that's where there's an opportunity to make money (CHA–CHING!), as long as they are *willing* and able to pay for it.

That last bit matters, **OK**? You may be **INCREDIBLE** at gaming. You might wipe the floor with absolutely everyone. But the grown-ups at home don't need you to play video games, so it's highly unlikely you'll get paid to do it. For now, anyway. There actually are jobs out there that involve – **AHEM!** – *testing* video games. And professional gaming is a real spectator sport!

You're also not likely to get paid to do things you should be doing anyway. Like brushing your teeth twice a day or doing all your homework. Or pulling your weight at home if there are some things you all help out with (like tidying up after yourself or helping to set or clear the table).

'NICE TRY . . . BUT NO.'

On the other hand, if you offer to do something extra, something really useful like making homemade Christmas cards or doing all the family gift-wrapping, you might just be in with a chance.

BONUS TIME: There are some jobs that will give you a 'bonus' based on your performance. In much the same way, you *might* be able to negotiate some extra money for things like improvements in grades or special achievements. But remember – money shouldn't be the *only* or even the *main* reason you do these things.

46

Wanting to do something because of what someone else says about you or what they give you is called **extrinsic motivation** (motivation that comes from the outside). But the best kind of motivation is **intrinsic motivation** (the motivation that comes from *inside* you). It's like when you paint a picture or get to a new level in a game because you *want* to. Because you *enjoy* it. When motivation comes from the inside, you work harder, do better, and your achievement is much more satisfying.

'WHAT DO YOU WANT TO BE WHEN YOU GROW UP?'

MONEY TOMORROW

Hands up if you've ever been asked that question. Grown-ups love it. But it's very annoying because it puts you under a lot of pressure and all the focus is on having *one* job or *one* career. But there are lots of things you can do to earn money in the future.

Whatever your interests and skills, there will be a job out there that is just right for **YOU** (*several* jobs, in fact!). If not, I'll eat my hat. I don't actually have a hat but I'll buy one just so I can eat it. Here's what you do to ensure I don't have to:

Think about the things that excite and interest you

↓

Things you are good at or can work towards getting good at

↓

And if you can do something really well that not many people can do, you're on to something

The annoying truth is that some jobs pay more than others. *Usually*, the jobs that pay more are jobs that most people find difficult to do or get into (they might require lots of training, which takes time and can be expensive too). I say usually because there are some jobs that will take lots of training and are really fun to do, for example in the arts and education, but are still not paid very well. Now, this isn't right or fair and it **TOTALLY** needs fixing. But it doesn't mean you shouldn't do these jobs. We *need* these jobs. And you should follow your passions. If you want more money than these jobs can get you, you might need to get yourself a side-hustle, but don't worry – we'll get to that later.

And you don't need to feel like you'll be doing one job for ever either. That isn't how the world works any more. In the past, people often took up a job and stuck with it for life (with some exceptions, of course!). Today, job-hopping is on the rise. So is the **gig economy.** This means **freelancing** – where instead of working with one employer, you do contract work for a bunch of different companies and individuals. It means you'll have to keep hunting down your next piece of work, but it gives you flexibility and variety.

Guess what. *I'm* a job-hopper. I left a fancy job as a City lawyer to become a children's author. I loved lawyering but I was working day and night and something was missing. I wanted my *time* back and I wanted to do something that made a *difference.* I thought long and hard about what that might be. Then it hit me. I've always loved writing and telling stories and talking way too much. Being a children's author means I get to do **ALL** those things and make a difference and the best part is: I'm in the gig economy! I fit work into my life just the way I want to and I'm having the **BEST** time. Seriously. You can do anything you like. The world's your oyster!

SPACE PILOT TO 3D-PRINTED FOOD CHEF YOUR JOB OF THE FUTURE

How we think about work is changing but the type of work out there is changing too. By the time you get out of school, there will be jobs there for the taking *that don't even exist today.* Imagine that. Jobs like:

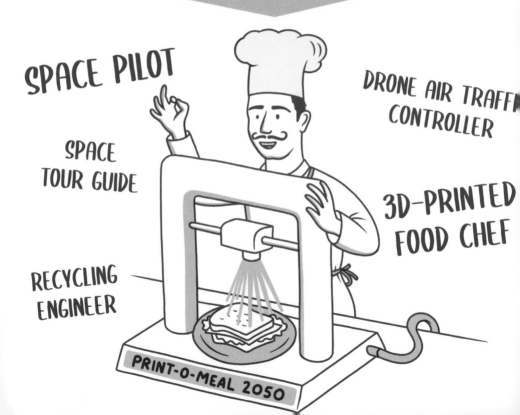

SPACE PILOT

DRONE AIR TRAFFI CONTROLLER

SPACE TOUR GUIDE

3D-PRINTED FOOD CHEF

RECYCLING ENGINEER

PRINT-O-MEAL 2050

Artificial intelligence (or AI) isn't science fiction any more either. Robots are already here. Some of them are in our pockets, like the virtual assistant Siri on the iPhone. Some of them are in our homes, like Amazon's Alexa.

'ALEXAAAAA, ADD ICE CREAM TO THE SHOPPING LIST.'

You've got 'smart homes' where the lights, locks and other things can be controlled remotely. There are cars that can drive and park themselves. There are surgical robots that help with operations! It's not just the big, funky stuff either. Netflix uses AI to analyse what we watch and recommend other shows and films we might like. And there is so much more to come.

'ALEXAAAAA, SET A TIMER FOR 20 MINUTES.'

So many things are changing. The best thing you can do today is to get ready for **change**. And the best way to do that is to get yourself some **skills**. Like **knowing how to learn**. Now, you might be thinking, 'How am I supposed to *learn how to learn*, that makes no sense at all.' But what it *means* is you need to become a **BOSS** at learning new things. This could be anything at all from learning a language or learning how to code to learning how to walk on a tightrope. You have to figure out what **strategies** work best for you. Maybe you like to read about something first, then watch people (in real life or on video) and copy them, then practise, practise, practise. Maybe you prefer to jump straight into watching or listening and practising. *What* you learn might change but the *learning* bit is the same (though you'll tweak it a little depending on what you're learning). Get good at *learning* and if you want to try something new, you know you can always work on it!

There are plenty of other useful skills you can collect, skills you can pop in your pocket and take with you from job to job. Here are a few juicy ones:

ADAPTING TO CHANGE:
You work in a factory making handmade thingamajigs. You **ROCK** at making thingamajigs. Suddenly, your boss announces you're going to be making thingamawotsits. You can't just go off in a grump or complain about it. You need to adapt and be flexible.

TEAMWORK

MAKING MISTAKES AND TURNING THINGS AROUND:
So you messed up. You were supposed to paint the thingamawotsit green and you painted it yellow. Easy to do. Don't be hard on yourself. Accept that it happened and think about how you can fix it.

WORKING WELL WITH OTHER PEOPLE:
You're not going to be able to make and sell that thingamawotsit all on your own. Be nice to the people you work with. Get to know them. If you make a good team, the thingamawotsit business does well and you *all* do well.

FIXING MISTAKES
✔

EMOTIONAL INTELLIGENCE:

This is about understanding your (and other people's) emotions and knowing what to do with them. If someone's upset about their thingamawotsit, can you listen to them? Be there for them? When *you're* upset or frustrated, can you tell you're headed down a slippery slope and can you reach out for help? Are you good at expressing yourself?

CREATIVITY:

Now your boss has given **YOU** the chance to design a brand new thingamawotsit! But uh-oh. You don't think you're very creative? Anyone can be creative. Come up with lots of ideas. Write them down or draw them, however silly they seem. Give yourself permission to be silly. Do this with a friend or even a whole team. Go for walks, listen to music, whatever gets you in the zone.

CRITICAL THINKING:

This is like doing a puzzle or problem-solving. You think things through. You've just been given **THE GREAT BIG HANDBOOK OF HOW TO MAKE THINGAMAWOTSITS.** Yeah but ... who wrote it? Why did they say what they said? Is there a better, faster, cheaper way to make thingamawotsits? That's critical thinking.

DECISION MAKING

DECISION-MAKING:

Decisions can be tough. Which socks do you wear for a big meeting? How many thingamawotsits should you make? What price should you sell them at? What you need is a good decision-making process. Where do you start? How will you think things through, weigh up the pros and cons? Do you need any more information to make a decision?

CULTURAL AWARENESS:

Your factory is in Apple Land but you might have some people from Pear Land working with you. People from Pear Land have lots in common with you but they might have some things they do differently. There might even be a few things you say or do here that are a bit … well, *rude* over in Pear Land! **OOPS.** The more you can learn about Pear Land, the better!

CULTURAL AWARENESS

And of course, if you want to be good with **DOSH,** you need to think about getting good at basic maths. We might have calculators and computers but we don't have them following us around all day (imagine!). You can get confident with numbers at school, but you can also find tons of amazing resources online, in books, magazines, websites, apps and more. If you're worried that you're rubbish at maths, *don't* be. It's just a question of practice. Don't let the numbers scare you or worry about making mistakes. Just take your time.

$$597$$
$$\times 7$$
$$\overline{4179}$$

$$84$$
$$+ 43$$
$$\overline{12}$$

PRACTICE CAN PACK A REAL PUNCH!

Getting good at something takes practice. A **LOT** of practice. Hours and hours and *hours* of the stuff. Weeks. Months. In some cases, *years.* Now, if that sounds scary to you, here's some good news: there **IS** a cheat code. Gamers, you know what this is, right? It's a code that lets you skip a level, power up in some way, or unlock hidden stuff in a game. And the ultimate cheat code for getting good at something (or at least, much better than you are now!) is *deliberate* practice.

Deliberate practice means looking at what you need to improve on and focusing on getting better step by step. Suppose you want to get really good at a magic trick. You can't work on everything all at once. Break it down into *all* the steps, *all* the tiny hand movements and take them one by one. Test it out and get feedback. Get a magician to spot where you can do better. Feedback helps with learning. Mistakes help too. Mistakes are your friend.

Like having a job or doing freelance work, being an **entrepreneur** with your own business is another way to earn money. The best part is, you don't even have to wait to get started. You can set up a business **RIGHT NOW.** (Though all the usual disclaimers apply, **OK?** Keep your head down, do your homework and keep going to school, of course!)

A STEP-BY-STEP GUIDE TO SETTING UP YOUR OWN BUSINESS

STEP 1 WHAT ARE YOU GOOD AT?

Write a list of all the things you're interested in and all the things you're good at or can get good at. It'll give you some inspiration when it comes to Steps 2 and 4!

STEP 2 WHO DO YOU WANT TO HELP?

Think about who you want to help. This is your customer. Your customer has to *need* or *want* something that you can give them and they have to be willing and able to pay for it. Who is that customer and what do they need?

STEP 3 DO SOME DETECTIVE WORK!

Who else is out there solving their problem or giving them what they want? How much are they charging? Are they doing a good job? What's missing? How can you do it better?

STEP 4 SOLVE A PROBLEM

Come up with an idea that solves their problem. If they want a fancy hat, make them a fancy hat. If they need a sip of cool lemonade on a hot day, make them that lemonade. Pick **ONE** thing to start with and focus on getting that right.

STEP 5 PLAN

Whip your notebook out and do some thinking. Where will you sell? A physical location? Online? How will you advertise? Do you need any money for materials or equipment? Have you saved up enough or do you need to borrow some from the grown-ups? Do you need any permits? Any training? Do you need a grandmother to sit you down and share her secret recipe for her seriously gooey cookies? Do you need a team?

STEP 6 TEST YOUR IDEA

Test your idea out on your target market. Get feedback and make your product or service even better. You might need to go back and update your plans from Step 5 based on what you've learned.

STEP 7 GET STARTED

Time to get started. But as you tweak your product or service and make it better and better, keep jumping back to Step 6 – test, get feedback, and improve. Keep doing that and you'll have yourself some very happy customers.

AMAZING TRAILBLAZERS

If this sounds like a lot of work and a long way to go, don't worry. There are lots of people to learn from and the key is to start small. The world is jam-packed with people who started small and built a business from next to nothing.

NAME: STEVE JOBS

COUNTRY: USA

COMPANY: APPLE

AGE WHEN HE SET UP THE BUSINESS: 21

WHY DID HE DO IT?

To build an affordable personal computer at a time when computers were super-expensive and really complicated.

WHAT'S THE STORY?

In 1975 Steve Jobs and Steve Wozniak got together in Palo Alto, California, to build a computer (Wozniak was good at this – he built his very first computer when he was just *13!*). They only sold a few computers but they used the cash to improve their designs. In 1977, their Apple II computer made them over $3 million in its first year and over $200 million just two years later. It wasn't always smooth sailing for Jobs. At one point, he was even chucked out of Apple. But he eventually returned as Chief Executive Officer (the CEO, AKA head honcho) and rolled out some of Apple's most iconic products including the iMac, the iPod, the iPad and the iPhone.

NAME: INGVAR KAMPRAD
COUNTRY: SWEDEN
COMPANY: IKEA
AGE WHEN HE SET UP THE BUSINESS: 17

WHY DID HE DO IT?

Because people really want affordable home stuff. And, as he later figured out, they *really, really* want affordable home stuff that is flat-packed so it saves space when it's transported and is cheaper too.

WHAT'S THE STORY?

When he was five, Ingvar sold matches to his neighbours. At seven, he discovered he could buy them in bulk and sell them for an even better profit. At 17, when his father gave him some money for doing well at school, Ingvar used it to set up a business – IKEA. He started off selling things like low-cost pens and picture frames and eventually moved into mail-order furniture, which turned out to be a big hit. One day, an IKEA worker decided to remove the legs from a table to help it fit into a car and that just happened to be the start of the flat-pack furniture phenomenon that made IKEA so famous!

NAME: ANITA RODDICK
COUNTRY: UK
COMPANY: BODY SHOP
AGE WHEN SHE SET UP THE BUSINESS: 33

WHY DID SHE DO IT?

To make cosmetic products that are completely natural and **NOT** tested on animals (very unusual at the time).

WHAT'S THE STORY?

Anita borrowed money to set up her first cosmetics shop. It was tiny – around 20 products with handwritten labels and five sizes of everything. Customers loved these cruelty-free cosmetics and the business grew and grew. Meanwhile, Anita's campaign work meant that testing cosmetics on animals was eventually banned in the UK. That's not all. Anita travelled the world to find raw ingredients for her products – she met and supported local growers and shared their stories, making sure they were paid fairly. She made a big success of her business and made a huge difference at the same time.

OK, SO THESE ARE GROWN-UPS. I HEAR YOU. BUT HAVE A LOOK AT *THESE* ENTREPRENEURS WHO STARTED SMALL *AND* STARTED EARLY.

NAME: TILAK MEHTA

COUNTRY: INDIA

COMPANY: PAPERS N PARCELS

AGE WHEN HE SET UP THE BUSINESS: 13

WHY DID HE DO IT?

Because one day, he really needed some books for an exam but he had left them at his uncle's house. He looked up delivery companies to have his books delivered to him the same day but they were so expensive. There had to be a cheaper way to do this!

WHAT'S THE STORY?

Tilak set up his own same-day parcel delivery service in Mumbai by teaming up with the city's famous 'dabbawalas'. These are local lunchbox delivery people who are known for being very organised and *very* reliable. By working with the dabbawalas, Tilak set up a super-speedy same-day delivery service and gave the dabbawalas a chance to earn some extra income. Tilak's uncle is now the CEO and runs the business while Tilak goes to school (Tilak joins in over the holidays and weekends). Papers N Parcels has grown so much – it has its own app and a team of over 150 employees and 300 dabbawala partners.

NAME: MIKAILA ULMER
COUNTRY: USA
COMPANY: ME & THE BEES
AGE WHEN SHE SET UP THE BUSINESS: 4

WHY DID SHE DO IT?

Because people love lemonade and she had a good recipe! And she could make that lemonade *and* do something good for bees.

WHAT'S THE STORY?

Mikaila knew a lot about bees, having been stung by them twice in a week when she was four. At first, she was scared of them but then she discovered how important they are. So she took her great-grandmother's recipe for flaxseed and honey lemonade and, with the help of her parents, turned it into a business that donates a percentage of its profits to organisations working to protect bees. She started by selling from a table outside her home and then supplying a local pizzeria, but within a few years, her lemonade was stocked in hundreds of stores around the USA.

NAME: MOZIAH BRIDGES
COUNTRY: USA
COMPANY: MO'S BOWS
AGE WHEN HE SET UP THE BUSINESS: 9

WHY DID HE DO IT?

You laughed at the fancy hat thing, didn't you? Well, Mo here set up his handcrafted bow-tie business because he couldn't find anything out there that matched his style or personality. The ones in the stores were always so boring.

WHAT'S THE STORY?

Mo set up shop on his grandmother's kitchen table in Memphis in 2011. He designed the ties and, to start with, his mother and grandmother helped him sew them (his grandmother taught him to sew too). Over time, Mo got into various stores and in 2017, he even got a one-year deal to make bow-ties for all 30 basketball teams in the NBA!

NOW IT'S YOUR TURN

Here are some business ideas **YOU** can get started on right away:

- Lemonade stand (or any kind of juice stand)
- Pet-sitting and pet-grooming
- Selling homemade food e.g. cakes or cookies (YUM!)
- Running errands for the elderly
- Selling gifts and gift baskets
- Musical performances (solo or as part of a band)
- Selling homemade greeting cards
- Making and selling candles
- Gift-wrapping services
- Upcycling things (making old things funkier and selling them on)
- Cleaning services
- Tutoring for younger children (if you're an expert in a subject, you can help teach someone younger)
- Gardening services (e.g. raking) leaves)
- Repair services (e.g. computer repair)
- T-shirt design and T-shirt making (or other kind of fashion design)
- Jewellery design
- Website design
- Stock photography (selling licences on websites like Shutterstock)
- Party-planning
- Vlogging on YouTube (but you'll need your parents' approval)
- DJing or MCing at children's parties
- Dog-walking

What else can you think of?

IN A NUTSHELL

✳ **THINK ABOUT YOUR GOALS.** A **vision board** can help. Stick it where you'll always see it.

✳ **IF YOU HAVE THE OPPORTUNITY TO EARN AN ALLOWANCE, ASK YOURSELF:** what do people need or want? What do *you* have to give?

✳ **THERE ARE SO MANY JOBS OUT THERE.** Think about what interests and excites you.

✳ **THE WORLD IS CHANGING.** Fast. So be a **BOSS** at learning new things.

✳ **GETTING GOOD AT SOMETHING CAN TAKE HOURS AND HOURS OF PRACTICE.** Sometimes weeks, months, or even years. The best kind? *Deliberate* practice.

✳ **ANOTHER WAY TO EARN MONEY IS TO BECOME AN ENTREPRENEUR.** It's all about people's needs and wants again. Test stuff out, see what people think, make some tweaks if you need to and do it all over again!

✳ **SETTING UP A BUSINESS ISN'T EASY** but there are lots of people who started small and did amazing things, including young people like you. Maybe you'll join them.

NOW, ONCE YOU'RE BRINGING IN THE DOSH, YOU'LL NEED TO KNOW WHAT TO DO WITH IT, WON'T YOU? SO GRAB YOURSELF A SNACK AND TURN OVER . . .

CHAPTER 3
HOW TO
SPEND IT

So, you've got some DOSH.

YESSS!

Now what? Where and how do you SPLASH the CASH?

First of all, less *splashing* and more *thinking*. Spending is about **choices**. With limited money, you need to decide where to spend it (as well as how much of it to spend and how much of it to save, grow, or give!). When it comes to spending, if you spend money on one thing, you can't spend that money on something else.

And yes, there's a fancy term for this: **Opportunity cost** – the value of the next best thing you give up whenever you make a choice. So, if you're in an ice-cream parlour and you've only got enough money for *one* scoop of ice cream, you can choose chocolate *or* strawberry. If you choose chocolate, you can't have strawberry. The opportunity cost of going for chocolate is the scoop of strawberry you have to give up. And vice versa.

Spending money is also about **priorities**. Some things are just more important than others so before you begin spending your dosh, you have to figure out what's most important to *you*.

THE FIRST THING TO ASK IS: IS IT A 'NEED' OR IS IT A 'WANT'?

'NEEDS' ARE MUST-HAVES LIKE FOOD, WATER, BASIC CLOTHES TO WEAR, AND A SAFE PLACE TO LIVE.

'WANTS' ARE NICE-TO-HAVES. THE LUXURIES. THE FUN STUFF. THAT PHONE YOU REALLY LIKE. THE JACKET YOU'D LOOK SO GOOD IN. THE MOVIE YOU WANT TO GO AND SEE BECAUSE EVERYONE IS TALKING ABOUT IT.

'Needs' come first. Someone's probably taking care of most if not all of your needs today, but tomorrow, that'll be *your* job, so you have to be able to recognise them. You don't want to spend all your money on that lovely coat, platform shoes and hair dye, but have no money left to eat for a week.

AM I BEING FOOLED BY TRICKSY ADVERTISERS?

Remember we talked about **skills** in the last chapter? Well, people who work in advertising are *very* skilled in making you think that a **want** is a **need**. They come after you in so many ways – from TV commercials and internet ads to billboards, the backs of cereal boxes, and sneaky appearances of products in movies. And they've got a whole bag of tricks in their toolbox.

TRICK NUMBER 1: Associations. Our brain likes to link ideas, images and even *feelings* together. If the Mr Scrumptious chocolate bar adverts all have a scene with creamy chocolate pouring down and a bunch of people just like you sharing a bar and having fun, then that'll slowly stick in your brain. You think of the Mr Scrumptious chocolate bar, you think 'CREAMY, DREAMY, MELT-IN-THE-MOUTH CHOCOLATE' and you *feel* relaxed, happy, like you're hanging out with friends. Clever advertising can create these links or **associations** in our minds.

TRICK NUMBER 2: Celebrities and influencers.
A common trick is to use celebrities or influencers in ads or movies or to get them to post about a product on social media. The idea is that if our heroes love a product, it *must* be good. But these celebrities have been *paid* to advertise those products. They don't necessarily *use* them! We're clever, right? We wouldn't fall for that kind of thing. Except that we do. All the time.

TRICK NUMBER 3: Fear. Nothing gets us moving like FEAR does. Advertisers know this. They magically change **wants** into **needs** by putting the fear into us.

'IF YOU DON'T USE THIS TOOTHPASTE, YOUR TEETH WILL ALL GO BLACK AND CRUMBLE AND FALL OUT OF YOUR MOUTH.'

Another kind of fear they play on is FOMO – Fear Of Missing Out. We *need* the latest supercool whatsit because it feels like *everyone else* has got one (or will get one very soon!) and we just can't afford *not* to.

TRICK NUMBER 4: Repetition. Advertising hits you again and again and again and again until it sticks in your head. Given a choice, we tend to prefer things we are familiar with because **FAMILIAR** = **TRUSTED,** safe. Also, amazingly, if you see or hear things enough times, you're more likely to believe that what they say is true. Over time, you'll probably start to *believe* that you really do need this product to make you happy, popular, organised, healthy, etc.

But it's not just advertising that influences us. It's also our role models – our heroes, our fashion icons, our friends. Yep, our *friends* too. It's not that they're standing over us, deciding what we like and buy. At least, I hope not! But we care about them and we care about what they think. We just want to be *loved*. So we keep buying things to make us feel better, cooler, more successful, more enviable, more loveable.

The thing is, **WANTS NEVER END.** I'll be happy when I get my ...

BIKE – TV – ART SET – HOLIDAY – JACKET – MOBILE PHONE – LAPTOP – CINEMA TICKETS – SHOES – GAME – BAG – SCOOTER – MUSIC TICKETS – TRAINERS – BAG – JEWELLERY – MUSIC – HEADPHONES

There will always be something nicer, newer and shinier around the corner. We can end up spending a *lot* of money this way and that can get quite dangerous if we don't keep an eye on it.

The best way to combat advertising and even peer pressure is to work on being **OK** with who we are, just the way we are. And being content with what we have. This doesn't mean you shouldn't have dreams. Dreams are important. But hooking your happiness on a **THING** isn't going to work. Once your basic needs are taken care of, happiness doesn't come from a thing. You can't open a box and find *happiness* sitting there. It comes from inside you. And as for your friends, if they're *real* friends, they won't judge you because you don't have a new pair of trainers or the latest video game!

YOUR SECRET WEAPON

Gratitude is your secret weapon in the war against wants that spiral out of control. The more attention you give to the stuff you've got and how lucky you are to have it, the less time you'll spend thinking about what's *missing* in your life. That's ultimately why we want to buy things – because it feels like something's missing and if we could *just* get those trainers, we'd be smarter, cooler, happier and everything would be OK. Being grateful *now* is like reminding yourself that there is no sneaker-shaped hole in your life. Everything's *already* OK.

So, every day, before you go to bed, write down three things that you're grateful for. Could be anything. Big or small as you like. Three things.

BUDGETING

Once you know your needs from your wants, you can get stuck into drawing up a **budget**. A budget is a **plan** for your money. It's got two main parts:

MONEY IN (income)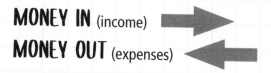

MONEY OUT (expenses)

What you do is you make a pretty table like this. Don't let it scare you. It's a really simple idea:

MONEY IN	EXPECTED	ACTUAL
Allowance		
Extra money earned		
Gift money		
Total		

MONEY OUT	EXPECTED	ACTUAL
Savings account		
Ice cream		
Movie		
Trainers		
Donation to local library fundraiser		
Total		

For **MONEY IN**, you note down all the money you think you have coming in this month. That's stuff like your allowance or money for chores (if you get any), gift money, money from a side-hustle if you've set one up, and, later, from a job if you have one.

For **MONEY OUT**, you do the same for all the things you plan to spend money on. You'll see there's a line for **savings** here and it's right at the top. It's not an **expense** but we'll put it here because it's a *very* good idea to stick to this little principle:

Pay yourself first. Instead of saving money that's *left over*, squirrel some away *before* you spend any. We're using the term 'saving' loosely here – it just means money you don't spend. Maybe you'll put it in a savings account or maybe you'll invest it somewhere. (More on that in the next couple of chapters.)

Once you've made your little table, you can compare your total **MONEY IN** to your **MONEY OUT**. Your **MONEY OUT** should not be bigger than **MONEY IN**. If it is, that means you're over budget.

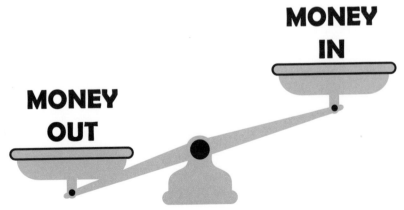

OVER BUDGET WARNING!

That means you're trying to spend money you don't have. **UH-OH.** You'll need to find a way to earn a bit more, slash that spending, or both. **TOP TIP**: If you can, do *both*.

Now, remember – these are all *expected* figures. As you go through the month, you'll note down your *actual* figures, so make sure you keep all your receipts! Maybe your expected figures showed you were over budget but thanks to your **GENIUS** plan of cutting back spending or bringing in some extra dosh (or both!), you're now *under budget*.

MONEY IN IS GREATER THAN MONEY OUT. YES. GO, YOU!

So now you can put that extra amount (the difference) towards your savings. Or give it away. Or roll it over into the next month. Whatever you decide to do, things are looking good. HIGH-FIVE.

BUT, A WORD ABOUT MAGIC MONEY

When we get hold of money that isn't earned and is unexpected in some way, like a gift or a note we find down the back of a sofa, we tend to treat it like MAGIC money. We don't tend to spend it on *boring* things like **needs** and we don't tend to do sensible things with it like saving it or investing it. Instead, we more often than not want to splurge it on things we might not need. But remember this:

THERE IS NO SUCH THING AS MAGIC MONEY.

It's just *money*. That money you get as a gift is the same as the money you work hard to earn. So you should treat it the same way and think carefully about how much of it to spend, save, grow and give.

WHEN YOU SPEND YOUR DOSH, SPEND IT RIGHT

When you're ready to start spending, you need to be savvy about it. Are you going to spend it all on short-term things like an ice cream or a trip to see a movie? They're great while they last, then **POOF**... they're over. Or are you going to spend it on long-term things that you can keep and reuse and enjoy over and over again – like a book or a game? You might also want to be careful with impulse buys, avoid fast fashion, and be wary of good offers that aren't *quite* as 'good' as they seem!

IMPULSE BUYS

Impulse buys are things we buy without thinking too much. Spur-of-the-moment decisions. They actually give us a little **ZING** of what feels like happiness. **WATCH OUT FOR THIS.** It's a slippery slope. A few too many of those and you'll run down your spending pot in no time. Ask yourself: do you really need this? If not, **PUT IT DOWN.**

Protect yourself against impulse buys with some good solid planning (shopping lists and budgets are your friend).

There are some children's bank cards out there that are tied to an adult's bank account. They can often be used from age six and they come with apps that let you track your spending, saving and even your giving. There's also a fixed amount that you're allowed to spend so you don't have to worry about going over budget.

But be careful. Bank cards are really useful but they make it so easy to over-spend. It's so quick and effortless that it doesn't even feel like spending. So it might be better to stick to cash sometimes. Cash is handy because you have to get it out of your wallet and count it. That gives you more time to think about what you're doing. You also actually see it disappear. **YIKES!** There's none of that with a bank card.

FAST FASHION

Cheap and cheerful clothing might sound like a good deal to you but you have to watch out. It might be cheap because it's lower quality. There are lots of shops that will do a great deal on clothes. They tend to have new things in *all* the time. Everything's cheaper so you feel like you're getting more for your money. But if it's poor-quality stuff, it just won't last and you'll be back at the shops in no time buying new stuff to replace it. You might even end up spending *more* in the long run.

It's also a massive waste and puts pressure on the environment. All that fabric from the clothes you chuck away that aren't donated or recycled end up in landfill (in 2017, *235 million* pieces of clothing were sent to landfill in just the UK!). Carbon emissions are a big problem too – the United Nations says the fashion industry uses up more energy than aviation and shipping put together. Unbelievable! And fast-fashion clothing is often made of synthetic materials, which can release up to *700,000* microfibres into the environment with every wash, polluting the sea and harming sea-life. **THINK OF THE FISHES!**

BEWARE OF THE NOT-SO-SPECIAL SPECIAL OFFER

Special offers are **EVERYWHERE.** To understand why they work so well, there's something you need to know about the human brain. It's *very* good at what it does but it was built a very long time ago and things have changed a little bit since then. See, the brain is designed to save energy. Because back in the day, we needed it for important stuff like fighting predators and hunting for food. We couldn't spend it all on thinking and decision-making, which, by the way, does use up a *lot* of energy. And *time.* Another precious resource.

So, the brain takes **short cuts** to help us make decisions. It does this even today, despite the fact we don't need to worry about sabre-toothed tigers or giant bears gobbling us up for their lunch! But when you're shopping, these short cuts can land you in trouble. Advertisers know this and they use it too.

The anchor in the sand … To save time and energy, when comparing things, our brain uses one of those things as an **anchor**. When you see a price tag with an old price crossed off and a new, lower price scrawled on the tag, the old price becomes an anchor. Instead of thinking about the price you'll pay in terms of the **opportunity cost** (comparing it to what you're giving up in order to buy it), it gets you thinking about what an amazing *deal* you're getting. Friends, **THIS IS A TRAP.**

Also, when it comes to marked-down prices, of course *no one* wants to believe a store would pretend to bump up prices so they can make a discount look like a discount, but the fact is, we all know some stores that seem to be holding neverending sales, right? It's a game. And it works.

THE CHEEKY DECOY

You might have seen a similar trap at the cinema when you try to buy popcorn. Ever seen three sizes that look something like this?

SMALL: £4.50   MEDIUM: £6.00   LARGE: £7.00

The medium price is the *decoy*, a distraction! You probably don't *need* the large popcorn, but you think, 'Why not – it's just £1 more. It doesn't make *any* sense to get the medium.' You're a sensible person so you make a sensible decision. And it's exactly the one they wanted you to make. By the way I'm using pounds here because I'm from the UK so I think in pounds! But you can swap in any currency – dollars, euros, yen, whatever it is that you use. These tricks work in every currency!

THE SUPPOSEDLY 'GOOD' BARGAIN

We're built to spot a bargain. We're tickled by signs like

 and

In fact, even *seeing* the word 'FREE' gives us that little ZING (just like an impulse buy). It's that powerful. We *love* a bargain. But is it really a bargain? If you don't need the item and weren't going to buy it anyway, the answer is NO.

The same rule applies to coupons and discount codes. Run the 'do you need it?' test. You'll often see coupons or multi-buy deals for perishable (things that don't last) items like food and guess what? That extra stuff often ends up in the bin. Heard of waste mountains? Mountains of food that's been chucked away? Yeah ... not nice. Pretty grim, in fact.

The bottom line is: STOP. THINK. Ask yourself: 'Do I really need this? And is this a good deal?'

PSSSST ... WANTS ARE OK TOO.

Provided you've taken care of your needs and you're doing some thinking about the future, *of course* you can splash out a bit once in a while! I'm not saying you can't ever do that. I'm not a MONSTER.

DO YOUR RESEARCH!

Shop around to compare prices at different stores. Compare similar products. Remember, supermarket own-brand products are often cheaper than branded stuff and you might find they taste the same or even better! Can you do a taste test at home? Get a branded product you always buy and a supermarket version. Then, get everyone at home to taste each one and guess which is which.

There's a difference between **PRICE and VALUE.** The price is what you pay for something. The value is what it's really worth to *you*. If you do a taste test and find that the supermarket's milk chocolate bar tastes better than the Mr Scrumptious chocolate bar, then even if it's cheaper, it's actually worth a lot more!

Check for customer reviews whenever you can. There are lots of review sites where you can see what customers think of a product. Remember not to take them all at face value though. There are some fake reviews – good and bad! – out there too.

SIDE-NOTE: STAY SAFE

When you're older and you're buying things online, make sure you have a secure internet connection and watch out for websites that look dodgy – spelling mistakes and security warnings might be clues. So are offers that sound too good to be true. If you click on one of those links, you might be letting a virus or a hacker into your phone or computer! **GULP.** Nobody wants that! Always check for a padlock symbol in the address bar next to a web address. If a warning comes up when you click on the padlock, *shut that site down!*

If a website asks you to save your card details, click '**NO**'. Be very careful with personal information, passwords and PINs. If these fall into the wrong hands, people can pretend to be you and *steal your identity*, borrowing and spending a lot of money in your name. This is why it's not a good idea to share things like your date of birth online.

IN A NUTSHELL

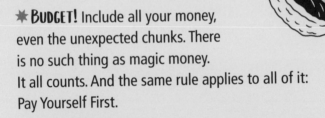

✳ KNOW YOUR NEEDS FROM YOUR WANTS.
Watch out for tricksy advertising
trying to turn your wants into needs.

✳ BUDGET! Include all your money,
even the unexpected chunks. There
is no such thing as magic money.
It all counts. And the same rule applies to all of it:
Pay Yourself First.

✳ AVOID IMPULSE BUYS – you're better than that!
Beware the not-so-special special offers.

✳ THERE'S A DIFFERENCE BETWEEN PRICE AND VALUE. Price is
what it says on the tag, but the value is what it's really worth to
you. Get good at looking for value.

✳ DO YOUR HOMEWORK. Compare prices and products.
Knowledge is power.

✳ WHATEVER YOU DO, STAY SAFE ONLINE. Never share
personal information and never ever share PINs and passwords.

RIGHT. NOW YOU KNOW HOW TO SPEND YOUR DOSH – COMING UP NEXT IS HOW TO SAVE IT ...

CHAPTER 4
HOW TO
SAVE IT

You're all set to save some money. Wonderful. Future you is going to LOVE present you. And because you've paid extra-special attention to the bit in the last chapter on the Big B (budgeting), you'll be thinking about tucking away your savings before you think about all those expenses. But where's the best place to put them? Let's see ...

QUIZ TIME:
WHERE DO YOU PUT YOUR SAVINGS?

A COOKIE JAR

B SOCK DRAWER/UNDER THE MATTRESS/IN THE FREEZER/ THAT KIND OF THING

C MONEY BOX

D BANK ACCOUNT

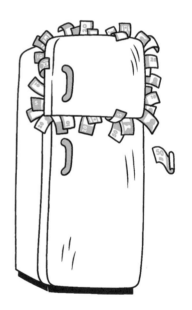

If you answered A to C, **YOU'RE FIRED**. The **CORRECT** answer is D – bank account. In fact, all the money you earn should be going into a bank, building society or credit union account (but we'll just say *bank* to keep it simple). When you need to spend that money, you can take it out as cash or spend it using a bank card. Depending on how old you are and the type of card you're using, you may need to ask someone older for help too.

BANK ACCOUNTS KEEP YOUR MONEY SAFE

Safe from *you* because you don't have to stop yourself sneaking into the cookie jar. And safe from *burglars* too. Burglars are in and out pretty sharpish after a break-in. They know **ALL** the usual hiding places. **OK,** you might be creative and hide your money somewhere unexpected. Trouble is, if your hiding place is *that* good, it's possible *you'll* forget where you put that cash when you really need it. Or something else might happen to it. In 2009, a lady in Israel had managed to save up $1 million in cash (yep – **$1 MILLION**), which she hid away in a mattress. One day, her daughter (who knew nothing about this) chucked the mattress out as part of a spring clean! Can you imagine?!

In some countries, a lot of the money in your account is protected by the government in case anything happens to the bank. In Australia, for example, that protection covers up to 250,000 Australian dollars per person per bank. You won't get that from your money box or sock drawer.

BANKS ALSO KEEP A RECORD OF MONEY IN AND MONEY OUT

These very handy records are **bank statements**. They let you keep on top of your earnings and spending and see how much money you've saved up. Money boxes are cute but they can't do this!

THE ANCIENT TEMPLES OF MESOPOTAMIA are, in a way, the world's oldest banks. They were super-safe (no one would DARE steal from the gods) and they stored things like grain and precious metals. They even gave out loans, including interest-free ones to people who couldn't afford the interest. They also kept amazing records on clay tablets. This 'cuneiform' writing is the oldest known writing in the world and dates back to 3300 BCE. Turns out that when humans first developed writing, it wasn't to write a poem or a prayer but to keep financial records!

BANKS HAND OUT FREE MONEY

Unlike money boxes, banks pay **interest**. This is basically FREE MONEY. You put £10 in a money box and 50 years later, it'll still be £10, except that *that* £10 might be old and out of date and, even if it isn't, it probably won't be worth as much any more because of a thing called **inflation**. You put that £10 in a bank account instead and it'll earn interest. So your money is literally GROWING while it sits in the bank.

Inflation is the steady rise in prices over time. In the UK, you could buy an orange for 17p in 1989, but in 2019 it cost 38p. So a £10 note stashed away 50 years ago would be able to buy a lot less today than it could back then!

UMM ... WHY DO BANKS HAND OUT FREE MONEY?

Banks pay you interest because they *use* the money you put in. It doesn't all sit there in an underground vault *(sorry, burglars)*. The bank only holds a small percentage of its deposits as cash. The rest gets loaned out to people who need to borrow it (people who are *over* budget). Yep, that's right, your money is probably actually being loaned to a stranger, but don't worry, it's completely protected. The bank charges that stranger interest on those borrowings and that **interest** rate can be quite high.

Here's how it all works. Imagine you've got 100 sweeties and you put them in a **SWEETIE BANK**. The bank promises to keep them safe for you. (They're safer here than in your house because you can't eat them and no one can steal them!) Now, when you're off doing other things, a Sweetie Monster comes to the bank and she **REALLY** needs some sweeties. So the bank lends her 50 of those sweeties (as you don't need them right now). But the Sweetie Monster has to promise to pay back all 50 sweeties (bit by bit each month.) *plus* 4 more sweeties as a **fee** for borrowing those sweeties in the first place! That's how banks make money (or ... umm ... sweeties!).

The Sweetie Bank pays you an extra sweetie for letting them use *your* sweeties to give a loan to the Sweetie Monster. That's your interest. And that's how your sweetie stash (your savings) grows in the bank without you lifting a finger!

THE SUPERHEROES, VILLAINS AND BEING A BORROWER

Your money can grow or get smaller in many other ways too, with the help of the heroes and villains of the banking world.

COMPOUND INTEREST – ONE SERIOUS SUPERHERO

Compound interest is big-hearted, generous, and my goodness it is FAST. There's some funky maths behind its magic but the good news is you don't need to understand the maths. PHEW. You just need to understand what it means. And what it means is that when you save money, you benefit from a **snowball effect**. Imagine pushing a snowball down a hill. You start with a tiny ball (that's the money you put in the bank). Thanks to compound interest, you roll it and roll it and, over time, it picks up more snow (that's

the **interest)** and becomes a bit bigger. Keep rolling and it gets bigger still, picking up even more snow. It gets bigger. And bigger … until it's a great big *boulder* of a snowball. But this snowball effect only works if you save the interest instead of spending it. So, letting your money *and* the interest earn even *more* interest = a chance to make some serious dosh.

WARNING: THIS IS NOT A GET-RICH-QUICK THING. For
compound interest to do its thing, **TIME** is the biggest factor. A decent interest rate matters too, of course, but time is critical. Time gives compound interest a power-up. This is why you should start saving *as soon as possible*. If you're reading this, you're one humungous step ahead because you can get started today.

QUESTION: Would you rather have **£1 MILLION** to spend *today* OR a magic pot of money, starting with a single PENNY, that doubles every day for 30 days (so Day One it's a penny, Day Two it's 2p, Day Three it's 4p etc.)?

Most people would choose the cool million.
Most people would be wrong.

In 30 days, that magic penny would have made you over **£5.3 MILLION.** If you had it one more day, it'd make you **£10.7 MILLION.** Unfortunately, magic pots don't exist, but if you save a small amount every day, you can actually end up saving lots. You know when you buy something and it's something like £5.95 and you have that 5p left over? Put that 5p towards your savings. Over time, it can really add up!

THE DARK SIDE OF COMPOUND INTEREST

All superheroes have flaws. **IRON MAN** is a genius, but he's also arrogant and can sometimes push people away. **WONDER WOMAN** is a powerful warrior but she doesn't understand much about ordinary humans and the modern world. **THE HULK** is amazingly strong but he struggles to control his strength. Compound interest has a flaw too. It's got a dark side. It can work *for* you but it can also work *against* you! **GULP.**

Remember banks charge interest on borrowings? Well, if you end up borrowing money when you're older and you don't have enough money to pay your monthly repayments in full, you'll be charged interest on the amount you don't pay back. Interest *compounds.* Before you know it, you'll have a *huge* borrowing bill. This is why, when you're able to get a **credit card** (a bank card that lets you spend borrowed money), **BE CAREFUL.** Interest rates for credit cards are super-high and you don't want those costs to snowball. The same applies to things like payday loans, which keep you going until you next get paid. Payday-loan lenders can also charge late fees and sometimes bump up interest rates if you don't pay their money back on time.

If that sounds scary to you, there's something even scarier out there: **LOAN SHARKS.** These are the biggest villains in town. Banks will only lend to people with 'good credit ratings' – people who they can trust to pay them back. If you don't have a good credit rating (because you've had trouble keeping up with bills or interest payments), banks may not be able to lend to you. When that happens, some people turn to loan sharks. Yep, they're as bad as they sound. They charge *spectacularly* high interest rates and can use bullying tactics to chase you down if you don't pay on time. **STAY AWAY** from these guys.

BEING A BORROWER

Now, all of those villains might seem a bit intimidating, but sometimes people do have to borrow money to plug a gap in their budget or to make a big but important purchase like a car or a house. It can bring up all kinds of not-so-good feelings. But it *is* normal. If you can get into the habit of saving and keeping control of those expenses, you may be able to avoid it and if so, great. But if you do have to borrow later in life, it's OK. You can use your planning wizardry to stay on top of your repayments and eventually get rid of that debt.

Just make sure you don't start to borrow too much just because it's so easy to get hold of loans and credit cards. Borrowing is *expensive* and not being able to make payments on time can affect your credit rating. And that makes it even harder and more expensive to borrow money later on. If you ever find yourself struggling with money, there's lots of help available – there are people who specialise in helping people figure out how to pay down their debts. There's no shame in asking for help. And, by the way, that applies to *everything* in life.

MORTGAGES

A mortgage is a special loan that people take out to buy property like a house or apartment. Property can be so expensive that this type of borrowing is actually very common. Someday, *you* might take out a mortgage too. And if you do, as with all kinds of borrowing, the important thing is to stay on top of repayments and focus on eventually paying that debt down. With a mortgage this is extra-specially important because if you can't keep up with repayments, the bank could take your home and sell it to get its money back! **GULP.**

DECISIONS, DECISIONS: WHICH ACCOUNT DO YOU GO FOR?

You've got your stash of money, but where do you put it? Well, there are **CURRENT** or **CHECKING ACCOUNTS** for everyday use – these let you take money out whenever you want but they come with very low interest rates. Then you've got **SAVINGS ACCOUNTS** with higher rates, but you'll often need to pay in a regular amount and keep your hands off the cash for longer.

Ideally, you should put all the money you get from allowances or gifts into a current account but move your savings to a savings account.

'OI! HANDS OFF!'

You might need a trusted adult to open a children's account for you. It works differently in different countries. In the UK, for example, most banks will let you run your own children's savings account from the age of seven, but children's current accounts are usually only available if you're between 11 and 18 (and some need you to be 16 or over). In the USA, you usually need to be 13 to run your own current account and your legal guardian often has to be a joint account holder until you're 18.

QUESTIONS TO ASK

Do they have online banking and an app you can use with the help of a grown-up?

Is the account free to use?

What's the minimum amount you have to put in?

What interest rate are they offering?

Which ATMs (cash machines) can you use to take out cash?

Are there any fees for taking cash out?

HOW SOON DO YOU NEED THAT CASH?

The best type of account for your savings depends on what type of saving you're talking about. If there's stuff you're saving up for in the near future like a hoodie or a new bike, you need to be able to get hold of that money soonish but not *right this moment*. So you'll want to put it in a savings account that lets you take money out when you want it.

Later on, you'll be saving up for some **BIG** goals like buying a car, an apartment, or a commercial flight to the moon! Whatever you've got your heart set on. **THAT** money can go in long-term savings accounts with even better interest rates.

THE UH–OH FUND

This is for when things go wrong. People sometimes talk about putting money away for a rainy day, but you might want to put it away for a *hurricane*. Now, hopefully, you'll never ever need this money. It's there **JUST IN CASE.** If you burst a tyre doing some amazing tricks on your new bike, a grown-up might not pay to have that fixed. That's where your Uh-oh Fund can help. Keeping Uh-oh money aside is a really good habit to get into. In the future, you might have some huge repair works or other costs you hadn't planned for. You might lose your job and need to live off your savings for a while. Your Uh-oh money can be a life-saver.

PENSIONS

Now, this is for **MUCH** later, when you start work, but another thing that can be a real life-saver is investing in a pension. A pension is a special savings plan that helps you save money for when you retire (that's when you stop working and skip off into the sunset). The age at which you're allowed to **retire** and start getting some of that money from your pension pot depends on which country you live in.

HOW TO SAVE MONEY SO YOU CAN SAVE MONEY

If saving is a good thing, saving *more* is even better. So see if you can slash any of your spending and put more money in your savings pot.

The family budget: Speak to the adults in your house to see if you can have a chat about your family budget. This is your glimpse into the future. *Fast-forward in time* and you'll have to think about all kinds of extra SUPER-FUN expenses to include in your budget:

ELECTRICITY BILLS   GAS BILLS   WATER BILLS   TRANSPORT COSTS

Yep. So much to look forward to. But *this* is why it's a good idea to become a money-saving whizz *now* before all of this kicks off! That way you'll have enough money set aside for all those things, and enough left over to have some fun too.

RENT
if you're renting a
house or apartment

THE COST OF ANY BORROWINGS
(like a mortgage to
buy a house)

TAXES
(this is money the government
collects to help pay for things lik
schools, roads and emergency
services — the more we earn, the
more we contribute)

HOW TO BECOME THE ULTIMATE MONEY–SAVING WHIZZ

TRACK spending – if you can see it, you can trim it.

MAKE SURE you don't use more water than you need.

Help **PLAN** meals and write shopping lists to avoid impulse buys.

Help **RESEARCH** things like big purchases, days out and holidays to make sure you're saving money wherever you can.

Help **RESEARCH** gas and electricity providers to find the best deals.

SWITCH to energy-saving bulbs and turn off the lights when you leave a room to save on electricity. bills.

CUT DOWN on transport costs by walking further.

Run some **HOME TASTE TESTS** to see if you can switch from some branded products to cheaper supermarket products.

Come up with **IDEAS** for **FREE** or cheap days out or evenings in. Things like walks, parks, museums, libraries, board games, making things, movie nights, and home karaoke (you don't need all the kit – the radio/YouTube and a hairbrush should do it!).

Learn how to **COOK**. Seriously. In time, this will save you a small fortune in bills for restaurants, takeaways and ready-meals and it's so much healthier. Have at least seven meals you can rustle up cheaply and quickly that look and taste professional. You're welcome.

SAVING: A GRAND PLAN

You know saving is a good thing. But *how much* should you be saving? The short answer is: **UMMM ... AS MUCH AS YOU CAN.**

Some people think 20 per cent of your **MONEY IN** is a good place to start but really, it's up to you.

SAVING GOALS

If you're saving up for something specific like that game, guitar or pair of trainers, there are two ways you can go about it:

1 If you need the money by a certain date, look at the cost and divide that by the number of weeks you have left to tell you how much you have to save each week to get there. (*I want to buy a £40 pair of trainers in 10 weeks ... so that's £40/10 = £4 a week!*)

2 If you have an idea of how much you can save per week, you could take the cost and divide it by this weekly savings figure to find out how many weeks it'll take to save up for your stuff. (*'A £40 pair of trainers. Hmmm, I think I could save £5 a week ... so that's £40/£5 = 8 weeks!'*)

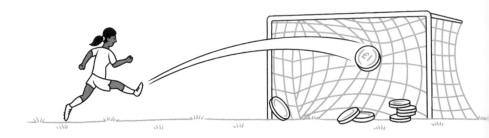

IT'S ALL ABOUT CHOICES

Any money you spend is money you can't save or grow or give.

Say you have your eye on those trainers that cost £40. They're a long-term thing – they'll last you until you wear them down or grow out of them.

> **FOR £40, YOU CAN HAVE FOUR TRIPS TO THE CINEMA AT £10 (TICKET + POPCORN + DRINK)**

OR

YOU CAN SKIP THOSE FOUR TRIPS AND USE THE £40 TO GET YOUR TRAINERS.

When you think about spending £10 on that first movie night, ask yourself: what do I really want? If my goal is to buy those trainers, is this ONE movie worth it or should I tuck that £10 away and save up for the trainers? Every little bit adds up.

THE SAVE-O-METER

Make yourself one of these to keep track of your savings goals. You can use any shape you like and colour it in as you save. Stick it somewhere where it's really in your face. Giving stuff up ain't easy. Maybe add in a picture of the thing you're saving up for so every time you see it, you remember WHY you're saving.

£40

£35

£30

£25

£20

£15

£10

£8

£4

£2

IN A NUTSHELL

✱ **SKIP THE SOCK DRAWER.** Savings should go in a bank account. In fact, all the money you earn should go in a bank (or building society or credit union) account. It's safer, it helps you keep track of what you've got and you get paid interest. **FREE MONEY!**

✱ **COMPOUND INTEREST IS A SERIOUS SUPERHERO.** Thanks to its power, your savings can snowball over time.

✱ **BUT ALL SUPERHEROES HAVE FLAWS** and compound interest has a dark side. It applies to borrowings too. If they snowball out of control, you can get in big trouble.

✱ **IF THINGS DO GET OUT OF HAND IN THE FUTURE,** there are people who can help. Reach out to them.

✱ **THERE ARE DIFFERENT TYPES OF SAVINGS ACCOUNTS AVAILABLE.** Look at what they offer and what their conditions are. Where you put your savings will depend partly on how quickly you need to be able to get them out.

✱ **ALWAYS PUT MONEY ASIDE FOR EMERGENCIES.** This is your Uh-oh Fund.

✱ **LEARN HOW TO SAVE MONEY** so you can save more money! Make a **PLAN** and stick to it.

SO FAR, WE'VE BEEN TALKING ABOUT SAVING MONEY BY PUTTING IT IN A STANDARD SAVINGS ACCOUNT. YES, IF YOU DO THIS AND YOU THROW IN THAT MAGICAL INGREDIENT *TIME*, OUR SUPERHERO BUDDY COMPOUND INTEREST WILL MAKE IT GROW. BUT THERE'S SOMETHING ELSE YOU CAN DO WITH THAT MONEY. YOU CAN *PROPERLY* WORK ON GROWING IT.

CHAPTER 5 HOW TO GROW IT

So. DOSH. You know what it is. You know how to earn it, how to spend it, and how to sneak some of it away into a savings pot so you've got something for the future. Savings are important. But there's something else you can do with some of that money to really GROW it. You can invest it. Before we get into what that means, there's something we need to clear up …

People often confuse wealth and income. Income is money coming in. But that's not the thing that makes you *rich*. Not really. It's what you do with that income. **Wealth** is the value of all your savings and assets (things like shares, property and valuable art) *minus* all the money you've borrowed (because that's not really yours and it needs paying back).

Now here's the exciting bit. If you're clever with your income (budgeting, saving and investing) – and you TOTALLY will be – then you can generate a *lot* of wealth over time. And the assets you invest in can bring in some dosh too.

NOW TAKE A STEP BACK AND IMAGINE . . .

When you read this chapter, imagine you've got a thousand pounds, or dollars, or whatever currency you use. I'm going to use pounds here as again, I think in pounds! Anyway, **YOU'VE WON A £1,000 PRIZE** for basically being amazing – **CONGRATULATIONS!** – and the *only* condition is that you've got to invest it. Investing just means you're going to put it somewhere that will help it grow. Thought I'd mention that bit before you go off to plan your little shopping spree! There are lots of ways to do this and while you read this chapter, I want you to think about what you'd choose. You don't have to put all your money in one place. In fact, as you'll see, you really shouldn't.

Company stocks (or **'shares'**) are one thing you can consider investing in. I know. Even the word 'stocks' sounds boring. But trust me, they're not. To understand why not (and what on earth they are!), have a look at this little story ...

A VERY CHOCOLATEY STORY

Remember how we said it's all about the choices you make? Well, here's one. If you have a bit of cash and feel like some chocolate, you can buy a bar of chocolate **OR**, you can buy (or **invest** in) a piece of the chocolate **FACTORY**.

If you buy a bar of chocolate, you'll probably eat it pretty soonish. Or maybe you'll save it for a special occasion or give it to someone else (aww!). But once it's gone, it's gone. And so is your money. So there you are: no money, no chocolate.

If you invest in a piece of the chocolate factory (we call this a '**share**'), your money's gone but you are now the proud owner of a share in an actual chocolate factory. **HOORAY.**

Over time, as the chocolate factory does well, it makes more money. And if it's doing so well that the money it makes is more than the costs of running the factory, we say it's made some **profit**.

MONEY IN
— MONEY OUT
PROFIT

Some of this profit is often shared with all the people that own a share in the chocolate factory (the **shareholders**). Yes, that means you. Wahoo! This share in the profit is called a **dividend**. It's paid per share so the more shares you've got, the more money you'll get. So now you can take *that* money and go buy *more* chocolate. Or more shares! Or spend it on something else, save it, or give it away.

Don't forget our favourite financial superhero, compound interest. Your savings snowball faster the bigger they get. So if you put the money you make back into your savings pot, your savings get bigger and so does the interest you earn!

CELEBRAAAAATIONS!

Not only that, if the chocolate factory is doing very well, lots of people will want a piece of it. They'll all rush to buy shares and as there are a limited number available, they'll increase in value. Including *your* share. So if you want to sell it, it'll be worth more than it did when you bought it.

CHA-CHING!

NOW, LISTEN VERY CAREFULLY.

Unfortunately, it isn't always that easy ...

What goes *up* can also come *down*. What happens if the chocolate factory doesn't do so well? In *that* case, things will look very, *very* different ...

DARK DAYS

There are all sorts of reasons why your chocolate factory might be struggling. Maybe people stop liking chocolate and stop buying it. It's **POSSIBLE, OK?** Maybe they're really worried about their teeth. **GULP.** Maybe the factory has lost its top-secret recipe. Maybe someone **STOLE** it. **GASP!**

Maybe costs have gone up and the factory is now *really* expensive to run. **MONEY IN – MONEY OUT = PROFIT,** remember? Well, the opposite of **profit** is a **loss.** If the company's losing money, that spells bad news for shareholders like you. You can forget about being paid a bit of extra cash.

And the value of your share? That's definitely going down as people try to get rid of their shares. Usually how it works is that stuff that *everyone* wants is worth lots and stuff that *no one* wants is worth *less*. And what *that* means is …

… **YOU'RE IN TROUBLE.**

Decision time: do you hold on to your share or do you sell it?

The best thing to do will depend on what you think will happen to your chocolate factory.

Are things going to get even worse? If so, you might want to sell your share and **RUN LIKE THE WIND.**

But wait. Is this just a bad patch? If you think business will pick up later, you might want to hold on to that share. You might even want to buy more while shares are cheap!

What you do will also depend on three things:

- How badly you need your money right now. (If you really do need it, it might be a good time to sell!)

- How long you can live without it. (If the answer is 'a very long time indeed', you could wait … if it's a good chocolate business, over time, it'll do OK.)

- How much **risk** you can afford to take …

WIBBLY-WOBBLY JELLY

Investing is a bit like standing on a massive wobbly jelly. Some jellies are just wobblier than others and this is true with investments too. **ALL** investments are risky and some are *particularly* risky. That's why you should **ONLY** invest money that you can afford to lose. So **DON'T** invest money you need for expenses. And **DON'T** invest money you need for your Uh-oh Fund. Otherwise, you might find yourself going wibble-wobble **SPLAT!**

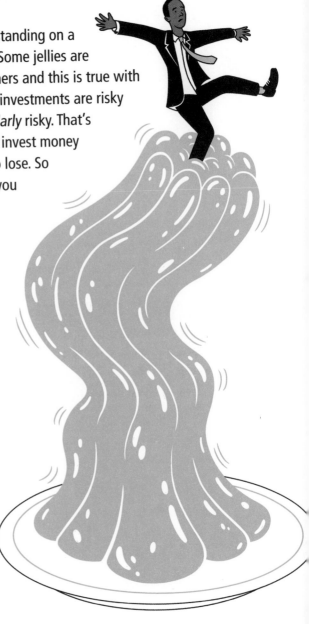

Now, no one would expect you to stand on that wobbly jelly for free – in return for all that **risk,** you get the opportunity for **rewards.** **IF** your chocolate factory does well, and **IF** you hold on to the shares, you could benefit from dividends (**IF** the company pays them) and a delicious little profit (**IF** you sell those shares at a higher price than the price at which you bought them). Yes, that's a whole bunch of **IF**s!

TOP TIP:
DON'T PUT ALL YOUR EGGS IN ONE BASKET
If you can, invest in a bunch of different things. Ideally, you'll invest in some that might do well when others are struggling. For example, you might want to invest some of that £1,000 in a chocolate factory and some of it a toothpaste factory or a chain of dentists! Lowering your risk like this is called **hedging.**

If you don't mind all the wibbly wobbliness, you can use your magical £1,000 prize money to buy shares in all kinds of companies – food, fashion, music, sports clubs, energy, technology, healthcare, thingamawotsits, *anything* really. But how? If you wanted to buy a bike, you'd buy it from a bike shop. If you're looking for shares, you'll find them on something called a stock exchange …

THE STOCK MARKET, BUBBLES AND THE MASTER INVESTOR!

The stock market is a special marketplace for buying and selling shares. The shares are traded on something called a **stock exchange.** There are 60 major stock exchanges around the world. The most important ones in the USA are the New York Stock Exchange (the NYSE), the Nasdaq and the NYSE American. The London Stock Exchange (the LSE) in the UK is one of the oldest in the world. Before the LSE was set up, people who wanted to buy and sell shares did their business in coffee shops around London!

The goal of any shareholder is to buy the stock, hold it for some time and then sell it for more than they paid for it. But prices constantly go up and down and so it's a risky business.
And if a whole country or region is going through a difficult time, share prices can fall quite suddenly because people get scared and start to sell their shares in all sorts of things. It can take a long time for things to pick up.

Sometimes, a particular thing becomes SO popular that lots of people want to buy it and soon *everyone else* wants to buy it too (**FOMO,** anyone?). And because there's a limited supply of shares, that pushes the prices right up.

This is exactly what happened with *tulips* in Amsterdam in the 1600s! At one point, you could buy a house in Amsterdam for the price of one rare type of tulip bulb. But it was a **bubble.** Eventually, the bubble **BURST** and tulip prices collapsed. A similar thing happened in 2000 with the **dotcom bubble.** People were rushing to buy internet company stocks in the late 1990s because they were so cool and exciting and nearly *everyone* was buying them and because nearly *everyone* was buying them, everyone *else* wanted to buy them ... **ANNNND** ... you can guess what happened. Yes, the bubble burst and the stock market **CRASHED**. This is precisely why you have to be *very* savvy when investing. And who better to learn from than the savviest investor of all ...

WARREN BUFFETT –
THE MASTER INVESTOR ...

Still not sure where you want invest your money? Well meet billionaire Warren Buffett. He started out selling chewing gum and magazines door to door and doing the newspaper round to make money as a child. He bought his first share when he was 11 but he earned 99 per cent of his wealth after turning 50. And that's a lot of wealth, by the way. In 2019, he was worth about $87 BILLION. Told you. A LOT of wealth.

How did he get there? Well, over time, he invested his money in companies he really believed in. Strong businesses with a solid business plan, not glitzy shouty ones that were all chat and no substance. Then he relied on our fabulous financial superhero, **compound interest,** to make his savings and investments snowball.

KNOW YOUR STUFF

In Ancient Greece, oracles like the famous Oracle of Delphi were priests or priestesses who were believed to have all the answers. Warren Buffett's nickname is the Oracle of Omaha because he lives in Omaha in Nebraska, USA, and people pay a *lot* of attention to what he has to say about how to invest. He knows his stuff, and he recommends that *you* know *your* stuff too.

Buffett says you need to be a **value investor.** That means you can't just look at the **price** of a share – you need to understand the **value** of the business (what it's *really* worth). Which means you need to *understand* the business. How else will you know how the company is really doing? How will you know if it's headed for trouble? Value investors are like detectives. They do some snooping to spot shares that are **undervalued.** The price might be low because no one wants the shares at the moment, but if it's a good business, a value investor sees that things will pick up one day!

Do you want to be a value detective? Hold on to that £1,000. You'll need to do some digging and you need to know where to look:

* **COMPANY WEBSITES:** see how well the company is doing and what plans it's got.

* **STOCK WEBSITES:** Google the stock to get a funky graph showing how the price has been changing. And look out for expert articles about the stock on websites like Motley Fool or Fool UK.

* **THE NEWS:** see what's happening in the world that might affect that business.

💡 BUT WATCH OUT

Past performance is **NOT** a guarantee of future performance. Anyone who's supported a winning football team knows this. They might have just won a big game but a mediocre performance or even a crushing defeat could be just around the corner. But that's OK. If they're a good team, you know they'll be all right *over time*.

FANTASY STOCKS!

Investing in real shares might be a little way away for you but you can always do a test run. Pick a company that you really like. Could be anything. Do as much research as you can on it. If it's listed on the stock market, you'll be able to look it up online and see how it's been doing. Invest your imaginary money in that company today. Then track how it does over the next few months. A year. Longer. Do this with a small bunch of companies. It's a bit like Fantasy Football but for business. Follow the news. Get used to thinking like an *investor*. Get some friends to do this with you and see how you compare!

THE BIG BANK OF BOREDOM

z^Z Z Z

How are you feeling about investing in shares? Still got that £1,000? Our little game isn't over yet. I've got more options for you! But that means stepping into the **BIG BANK OF BOREDOM** and meeting some serious contenders for the most **BORING** names in the history of the world …

FUNDS

If you liked the sound of shares, you could take your magical £1,000 and buy individual shares or you could invest in companies called **funds,** which invest in lots of different things for you. They won't win any prizes for fun-sounding names but they've usually got their ear to the ground to sniff out the best investments. No guarantees though! If it was *that* easy, *everyone* would do it.

Our friend, Warren Buffett, is a big fan of **index** funds. An index basically measures the value and performance of a whole bunch of companies. If companies are different ice-cream flavours, an index is a mega-sundae that's made up of *all* the best flavours! Like the S&P 500, which is an index of 500 big companies in the USA. Index funds track these indexes so investing in one of these is like investing in all of those companies. It's one way of keeping your eggs in lots of baskets and it'll cost a *lot* less than investing in all of those companies individually.

CERTIFICATES OF DEPOSIT

And you didn't think *anything* could sound more boring than stocks and shares! **HELLO,** certificates of deposit (we'll just say CDs because that's a mouthful!). These are a bit like a savings account where you put in a chunk of money and earn interest on it. **BUT** you can't touch the cash for a fixed period (usually between six months and five years) or you'll have to pay a **BIG** penalty. So this is *not* the place to put your Uh-oh Fund but it's good for savings you don't need for quite a while. Interest rates are better than normal savings accounts and CDs are considered safer than stocks or bonds, as you'll almost always get your money back.

Hold on a second. **BONDS?!** Wondering what they are? Well …

BONDS

BORING name, but at least it's short and sweet, eh? Simple idea too. Investing in **bonds** is like lending money to a government or to a company like our chocolate factory. They borrow your cash (and cash from lots of other investors like you!) and promise to pay it back with interest. That's right. This is where *you* get to be the big cheese, using some of your magical £1,000 to help the chocolate factory out. Again, it's like putting money into a savings account where you can't touch your money until a certain date. Except that you get a better interest rate and you really do have to think about **risk** and just how wobbly the jelly you're standing on might be!

WIBBLE WOBBLE

Help is at hand too. Bonds are rated by credit-rating agencies who tell you whether they think a company or government can be trusted to pay you back. The lower the rating, the riskier (and wobblier!) the investment but the higher the **interest** you'll get.

WARNING: BEWARE OF FUNKY COMPLICATED THINGS!

Credit-rating agencies can sometimes make mistakes. That's what happened in the 2008 financial crisis when agencies gave some bonds good ratings when they were actually very dodgy investments. You see, the bonds that the banks had come up with were so complicated that even the credit agencies didn't know what they were looking at. It all *seemed* OK so they stuck on a gold star when they should have stuck on a big red **WARNING** label!

If an investment is too tricky to understand and no one seems to be able to explain it to you, it might be worth side-stepping it altogether ...

PEER-TO-PEER LENDING

This is basically *people* lending to people over the internet (**I KNOW** – why don't they just call it *that* instead of using fancy words like 'peer'?). It cuts out the bank and makes borrowing easier and cheaper for individuals and small companies (cheaper because, unlike banks, lenders like *you* don't have huge running costs to cover!). So you get to be the big cheese again and, just like a bank, you make more money by charging interest. It's risky though – people are vetted by lending platforms but there's always a chance you'll meet a Sweetie Monster who can't keep up with sweetie payments and you'll lose everything you loaned them!

CROWDFUNDING

Another boring name from the Big Bank of Boredom but **crowdfunding** is actually quite interesting. Again, it lets individuals or companies skip the banks and raise money online. Some platforms let you buy shares in small companies in return for your cash. Others offer 'perks' instead like a cheaper, early version of a product. Perks won't really *grow* your cash so it's more a feel-good/support-a-business type of investment (but those are important too, so if you want to invest some of your £1,000 here, that's perfectly **OK!**).

THEN THERE'S THE FUN STUFF

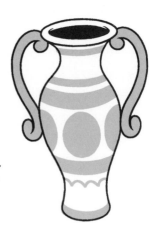

LIKE ANTIQUES.

OR ART.

OR PROPERTY.

OR COMMODITIES LIKE GOLD.

Fancy using your magical £1,000 to invest in any of these? They might become quite valuable over time. Take art, for example. Van Gogh apparently only sold one painting in his lifetime and that didn't sell for very much at all. Now, his paintings are worth millions!

But you need a lot of luck in this business. Sure, some people have found some real gems among their family heirlooms, but don't pin your hopes on that happening. And while you *may* have discovered the next Banksy or van Gogh, JUST in case you haven't … always **spread out** your investments. Again, you can buy these things yourself or you can invest in funds that invest in this stuff for you. It's often easier and much more affordable to do it that way.

CRYPTOCURRENCIES

Remember these from Chapter 1? There's not just Bitcoin, there are more than 2,000 cryptocurrencies in circulation.

In 2010, Laszlo Hanyecz, a man in Florida, bought two Papa John's pizzas using 10,000 bitcoins. At the time, they were worth about $40. Five years later, 10,000 Bitcoins were worth over $2.4 million. By 2019, they were worth over **$80 MILLION.** That's some *expensive* pizza. Laszlo probably should have held on to those Bitcoins!

Warning:

As we've talked so much about Warren Buffett, I should probably mention that he isn't keen on cryptocurrencies like Bitcoin! Unlike company shares where you can study the company, see how it's doing, and figure out the share's true value, Warren says that Bitcoin doesn't have any value in itself. Its price goes up if people keep buying it but you can't tell if it's really worth that much. And if people start to sell and sell and sell, those prices will come right down. Well, that's Warren. Others disagree and think it's very exciting and a thing of the future! You'll have to decide for yourself where you think it's headed. No one knows for sure. I know. I'm **SO** helpful.

SO WHAT DID YOU DECIDE TO DO?

See any investments you like the sound of? Were there some that sounded more interesting than others? Did you decide you'd put most of that £1,000 in one type of investment and spread out the rest? Did you split your cash up evenly? Or did you put lots in one place, then a little here, and a little there? Well, whatever you did, you just came up with an **investment strategy!**

So far, we've been playing with fictional money but one day, you'll have more money of your own and you can decide how much of it to invest and where. You'll be coming up with actual real investment strategies for actual real money!

IN A NUTSHELL

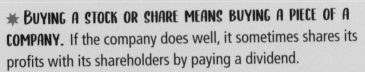

✳ **INVESTING YOUR MONEY** can get you an even higher rate of return than just saving it.

✳ **THERE ARE LOTS OF DIFFERENT WAYS TO INVEST,** including stocks, bonds, certificates of deposit, as well as things like art, property, and cryptocurrencies.

✳ **BUYING A STOCK OR SHARE MEANS BUYING A PIECE OF A COMPANY.** If the company does well, it sometimes shares its profits with its shareholders by paying a dividend.

✳ **IF A COMPANY'S DOING WELL, EVERYONE WILL WANT TO BUY A PIECE OF IT** and the price of those shares will go up, up, up, which means your investment is worth more and you'll get more dosh if you sell out.

✳ **IF A COMPANY DOES BADLY, THE PRICE OF THOSE SHARES WILL FALL** and so will the value of your investment.

✳ **BILLIONAIRE WARREN BUFFETT SAYS YOU SHOULD LOOK AT THE VALUE OF A COMPANY** when you invest. Invest in good businesses. They're keepers!

✳ **KNOW YOUR STUFF.** This rule applies to *everything*. You need to know what you're investing in! If something's too tricky to understand, it's probably best to steer clear.

✳ **WITH ALMOST ALL OF THESE INVESTMENTS, THE VALUE CAN GO UP AS WELL AS DOWN,** so remember: **EGGS, BASKETS** – lots and lots of baskets!

OK. THAT'S A LOT OF TALK ABOUT EARNING, SPENDING, SAVING AND GROWING YOUR DOSH. NEXT, IT'S TIME FOR THE GOOD STUFF. GIVING IT AWAY . . .

CHAPTER 6
HOW TO
GIVE IT

We've come a long way. You're all set to bring in the dosh, spend *wisely* in line with your budget, and you know you need to put some of that good stuff away to save and grow. You know that WEALTH is the thing to aim for, not just a good income. Now, the more wealth you have, the more you'll be able to *give*.

WHY GIVE?

Seriously? Because it's GOOD TO GIVE and you're a good human, aren't you? If you've got your mitts on this book, chances are you're already way better off than the overwhelming majority of people in the world. There's a lot of inequality and injustice out there. People are struggling with really basic things like having enough food to eat or being able to get an education or access to medicines. Some people don't even have a safe place to call home. This *planet* is struggling. We have whole ecosystems that are in serious trouble. These challenges look big and scary but there is a way forward. There are groups and organisations out there working to make the world a better place, step by step, and we can do *our* bit to help them too. By GIVING.

Giving is good and it FEELS good. I'm not saying this is why you do it but it's a very nice side-effect. When you give, your body actually releases feel-good chemicals called endorphins. It's that zing of happiness again — the warm, fuzzy feeling of actually *doing* something and *making a difference*. Humans are social animals. We're wired to care about and to help each other. Aren't we lovely? Well, *some* of the time ...

GIVING MONEY

WHICH CAUSES SHOULD YOU SUPPORT?

Well, it depends. What do you believe in? What kinds of things do you care about? What do you think is wrong in the world? What makes you *angry*? What gets RIGHT up your nose? What makes you so sad your heart hurts? Maybe it's just something you hear about that really pulls you in. There are hundreds of thousands of charities and organisations out there doing some good stuff and they touch on all kinds of things:

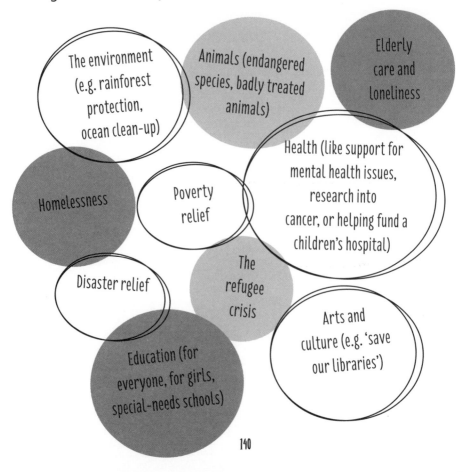

The environment (e.g. rainforest protection, ocean clean-up)

Animals (endangered species, badly treated animals)

Elderly care and loneliness

Homelessness

Poverty relief

Health (like support for mental health issues, research into cancer, or helping fund a children's hospital)

Disaster relief

The refugee crisis

Arts and culture (e.g. 'save our libraries')

Education (for everyone, for girls, special-needs schools)

When you find a cause that means something to you, see who's doing some work in that area. Ask yourself: do you want to support a *local* charity? How local? A super-local community thing? Or maybe a different country entirely? Or maybe you want to contribute to solving a BIG global problem? There are no right or wrong answers. It's your money, it's up to you!

WHICH SPECIFIC CHARITIES SHOULD YOU SUPPORT?

Do some detective work. Snoop around charity websites to see what they've been up to and what they say they're going to do next. Look up any videos they have about who they are, what cause they champion and what they're doing about it. Look up ratings and reviews. Look for *anywhere* people are talking about the charity or organisation and their experience of them.

QUESTIONS TO ASK YOURSELF:

Can they explain what they believe in and what they do in really simple terms? REEEALLY simple. If they can't and it's all wishy-washy and cute and cuddly but you can't quite put your finger on it, it's probably NOT the one to choose! This is true for any investment and *giving* is an investment in the world you live in.

Are they legit? Sadly, this is a fair question. There are some organisations that are basically scams. Horrible, isn't it? They say all the right things but the work just isn't happening. Or it is happening but it really isn't up to scratch. Sniff those out and stay away from them!

What are their goals and how are they getting on with them? You'll want to support an organisation with a proper **PLAN.** Real steps they can take and are taking. How are they measuring how well they're doing? You want to know that they're doing some proper research and making sure they meet their goals.

What can your dosh DO? Some charities and organisations actually list what different sums will get you.

£3 A MONTH COULD PROVIDE A
THERMAL BLANKET TO KEEP A
REFUGEE WARM

£15 COULD PROVIDE SCHOOLBOOKS
FOR 50 REFUGEE CHILDREN TO HELP
THEM CONTINUE THEIR EDUCATION

Like anything else in life, the more money you plan to put in, the more research you'll want to do.

HOW MANY CHARITIES SHOULD YOU SUPPORT?

You probably want to focus on up to five to really get the most out of your giving. You don't want to spread yourself too thin. If you had £50 to give, you could give that £50 to one cause or you could give 1p gifts to 5,000 charities. You'd be supporting more charities in the second case, but there's not a lot they can do with those pennies. That's not to say they don't add up and, yes, *every little counts*, but if you have a whole £50 to give and there's a cause you want to do something about, you might want to put as much into it as you can!

HOW TO GIVE MONEY

You might be thinking about a one-off gift to a cause. **OR,** you might decide to give a regular amount every month or year, a bit like the way you set aside an amount to save. You might even decide to give away a *percentage* of all the money you earn.

IF YOU CAN, MAKE GIVING A HABIT. GO ON. WORK THAT GIVING MUSCLE!

Regular donations work well for causes that you really care about. On top of that, you might want to think about keeping a chunk of money aside for stuff that comes up out of the blue like an appeal for a sudden natural disaster. Think of it as an Uh-oh Fund with a twist. Instead of being a fund for you if *you* get in trouble, it's a little fund you're keeping to help someone else out.

HOW MUCH DO YOU GIVE?

So Warren Buffett has pledged to give away 99 per cent of his fortune and that's a **LOT** of money. In fact, in 2010, Buffett and his billionaire buddies Bill and Melinda Gates set up The Giving Pledge, which was all about encouraging billionaires to give away more half their wealth to charitable causes. So far, over 200 have taken the pledge and they come from all over the world! How amazing is that?!

Now, that's **BIG MONEY** but giving doesn't *have* to be that big. Every penny you give is a penny you've decided not to spend or save or invest. Just making that decision to give it to someone else – that's *generous*. No one can take that away from you. Start wherever you're comfortable. No amount's too small. Maybe one day you'll go big too!

THE BIG GIVERS' HALL OF FAME

ANDREW CARNEGIE – When Scottish-born Carnegie sold his steel business in 1901, it made him one of the richest men in the world! He used his wealth to do lots of things, like building just over 2,500 public libraries. By the time he died in 1919, Carnegie had given away **90 PER CENT** of his fortune (worth billions today!).

J.K. ROWLING – You might know this author from her famous *Harry Potter* series but what you might not know is that she's also a big giver. She's given away millions of pounds to support causes like medical research and single-parent families. Her charity, Lumos, helps children in orphanages around the world find their family (and if you're a *Harry Potter* fan, you'll know that it's named after a spell that brings light to dark places!).

AZIM PREMJI – Premji is a tech billionaire and he's already given away over **£16 BILLION** of his wealth to help improve schools in India (especially in rural areas) and the lives of street children. Imagine if you had that kind of money to give away. What would you do with it? Premji's got a real soft spot for education. What causes mean that much to you?

TONY ELUMELU – This Nigerian investor and businessman has done so much to support the continent of Africa. In 2015, he decided to give 10,000 African entrepreneurs roughly £8,000 each to help them set up their own business. In 2017, he gave nearly **£400,000** to Sierra Leone to help people affected by the floods and mudslides.

GOOD SPENDING

Wayyyyy back when we were talking about spending, we talked about **choices.** One choice to think about is *who* you buy from. Spending is a kind of **POWER.** *Where* you choose to spend matters.

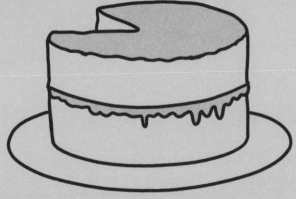

SHARING SOME OF YOUR CHOCOLATE CAKE

But before you can spend your money, you'll have to pay your taxes! Once you have that dream job and you get your first pay cheque, you'll see a slice of your pay **DISAPPEAR.** And if you do any extra work outside of that job, or work freelance, you'll have to declare it and pay tax on that money too. That's a portion of your hard-earned money gone – **POOF.** But it's important that this happens. See, the money you earn is like a chocolate cake. You just don't get to keep **ALL** of the chocolate cake (that would be greedy). Instead, you have to give a slice of it to the government as tax. If your cake is **TINY,** you don't have to give anything at all. But if your cake is **HUGE,** you give a bigger slice than if your cake is just medium-sized.

So what does the government do with that tax money, anyway? Well, that money helps to build and maintain roads, hospitals, schools, parks and libraries. It makes things like the emergency services possible. And it means we can *all* benefit from all of these services no matter how big or small our chocolate cakes might be. So, when the time comes, **PAY YOUR TAXES** – they make a **HUGE** difference to the community we live in.

COMPANIES THAT CARE ABOUT *FAIRNESS*

With all the stuff you buy, someone somewhere has been growing the raw materials used to make it (like the cocoa beans in your chocolate or the cotton in your T-shirt). Think about that someone and their family. They deserve a fair wage and safe working conditions, don't they? Well, your spending choices can help make sure they get them. When you're shopping, look out for products with 'fair trade' stickers – these stickers certify products and they tell you that the company behind them is working to make trade fairer.

COMPANIES THAT GIVE A PERCENTAGE OF THE PRICE OR THEIR PROFITS TO GOOD CAUSES

They might do this for a specific product or they might do it for everything they sell. If you were going to buy the thing anyway, it's a nice, easy way of *giving* at the same time. When you spot a company that does this, find out which causes they support.

BUY THE GOO

Some supermarkets let you donate food to foodbanks when you buy online. Some have a box in-store where you can pop donations. Or you might be able to take some 'impulse buys' out of your trolley and use some of that money to donate instead.

COMPANIES THAT SOLVE SOCIAL PROBLEMS

Some companies are literally built to do good in the world. Maybe they've been set up to train and employ people who find it hard to get work. Maybe they're a water filter company that also helps provide affordable safe water in places where it's badly needed. Support these companies and you support the causes behind them.

CHARITY SHOPS

Shopping at charity shops is another way of giving. Charity shops put their profits towards the charities they are connected to (but remember, **profit** is what they end up with *after* they deal with all the expenses of running the shop, and those might be quite high!). An added benefit of charity-shop shopping is that you're helping to reuse and recycle stuff that would otherwise end up in landfill, so you're doing your bit for the environment too!

ROM GUYS!

GOOD INVESTING

When you think about investing your cash, look at investing in companies that promise to respect things like human rights, animal rights, and/or protecting the environment. I **KNOW.** *All* companies should be doing this, right? Sadly, that's just not the case. But you can find some that do.

GOOD WORK

You can do good and *give* when you earn by trying to get a job at a **GOOD** company. One that cares about fairness and the environment, one that does something good in the world. If you set up your own business, you can make sure it's a **GOOD** business. Maybe you'll make your products in a place where people really need the work. Maybe you'll set up a business that helps people cut down on single-use plastics. LUSH does this by making and selling packaging-free soap bars and cosmetics (and, by the way, they also donate to environmental causes). Or maybe you'll come up with a business that helps other people set up businesses and become financially independent. Like Muhammad Yunus did with his Grameen Bank.

MUHAMMAD YUNUS, GRAMEEN BANK, BANGLADESH

In the 1970s, Yunus noticed that there were people in Bangladesh who wanted to set up businesses to sell their crafts and skills and get out of poverty but who couldn't get a bank loan. That's because banks were too worried they wouldn't be able to pay them back. Yunus decided to help by lending his own money to a group of 42 craftspeople, without charging any interest. They were tiny loans, really — each person only needed about £20 pay for their raw materials. The system worked! So Yunus set up Grameen Bank, which specialises in **micro-credit** (credit means a loan and micro-credit just means ... yep, you guessed it ... a TINY loan).

Yunus's microfinance project started small but Grameen Bank has now given loans to over 9 million borrowers in Bangladesh (97 per cent of them women!), helping them to set up their own businesses and support their families. Yunus and Grameen Bank were awarded the Nobel Peace Prize in 2006 for all their work. Now, there are even branches in countries like the USA because, as we know, people all over the world have trouble getting access to credit. And *no one* wants to get mixed up with loan sharks if they can help it!

IF YOU GIVE, GIVE IT YOUR WAY

You should never feel pressured into giving money. There are some causes and campaigners that will use your feeling of guilt against you. But isn't it **SO** much better to give from a place of feeling happy and generous than to give because you're made to feel like you're a terrible person if you don't?! If you're going to give, **YOU** decide when. **YOU** decide who you'll give to and how much. No amount is too small, no matter what anyone tells you, and there are so many ways you can give too – it can be a regular thing or a one-off. You can even keep a chunk aside for causes that crop up out of the blue. Whatever you choose to do, it has to come from *you*.

GIVING TIME

Right now, you might not have much (or any) money to give. That's **OK** because the one thing you do have is **TIME**. Even if you can't donate money, you can donate your time and your enthusiasm towards a cause that you really believe in. You do this by **volunteering.**

When deciding *where* to volunteer, just use the same process we used for deciding where to put your money. Think about the causes that matter to you and see what organisations are out there. There are some things you might be able to do right away. Is there something your school needs? Is a local library in need of support? Is there a soup kitchen you can help out at? Maybe you'll give your time towards raising awareness about issues like the climate crisis. You can do this alone or you can team up with other people to make an even *bigger* impact.

IN A NUTSHELL

* **THERE'S A LOT WE CAN DO TO MAKE THE WORLD A BETTER PLACE.** Giving is good (and it feels good too).

* **THERE ARE SO MANY CAUSES YOU CAN SUPPORT.** Choose the ones that really pull you.

* **SEE WHO'S OUT THERE DOING GOOD THINGS,** but do some detective work! Make sure the charity or organisation is legit and effective and make sure you know what your dosh can do for them.

* **SUPPORT BETWEEN ONE AND FIVE CHARITIES MAX** so you don't spread yourself too thin.

* **WHEN YOU'RE OLDER, SOME OF THE MONEY YOU EARN WILL BE TAKEN AS TAX.** If the money you earn is a chocolate cake, tax is a slice the government takes from that cake. If your cake is tiny, you won't pay anything. If it's big, you'll pay lots.

* **TAXES ARE IMPORTANT BECAUSE THEY HELP THE GOVERNMENT** fund things like schools, hospitals and the emergency services.

* **SPENDING = POWER.** When you **spend,** spend with companies that are the **GOOD GUYS.** That way, you *give* every time you spend.

* **WHEN YOU INVEST, INVEST IN THE GOOD GUYS.** Maybe even choose some funds that look for financial *and* social/environmental returns.

* **WHEN YOU EARN, EARN IT IN A WAY THAT MAKES A DIFFERENCE.** Work for companies that do good. Set up *businesses* that do good.

* **GIVE BECAUSE YOU WANT TO. AND REMEMBER – YOU** decide how much you're comfortable giving and who you want to give it to. Every little counts. Start small today but, who knows, you could be a **BIG GIVER** some day in the future!

* **YOU CAN GIVE MONEY** but you can also give your **TIME.**

WHAT'S NEXT?

SO. THAT'S IT.
IT LOOKS LIKE YOU'RE ALL SET ...

You know **ALL** about dosh. Well, all you need to know to get started, anyway. There's *plenty* more you can learn if you want to but we've got the basics ironed out, haven't we? You know how to make it. You know you need to make some choices about what you do with it and that means prioritising the important stuff over the come-on-you-*know*-you-really-don't-need-this stuff. You get the difference between needs and wants. You can sniff out a dodgy deal when you see one and you're totally **NOT** falling for all the sneaky tricks those clever advertisers have up their sleeves. Besides, you've got your own secret weapon in the fight against wants that spiral out of control: you know how to be happy with what you've got! So, **HA**, advertisers! Do your worst.

You're also a whizz at planning out a budget. You're going to make sure you don't go over budget but if it looks like you might, you'll slash that spending or find ways to make a bit more cash to cover the gap. In the future, you *may* have to borrow money. But you'll be super-focused on paying it back and **WHATEVER YOU DO**, you **PROMISE** to stay away from those nasty **LOAN SHARKS**.

You know you need to make a habit of tucking some money away as savings. And you're all set up with tons of ideas to save more money so you can actually *save* more money. You know where those savings go too, don't you? Stuffed under the mattress, right? **WRONG.** They go in the bank. There are tons of bank accounts to choose from (and savings accounts will nab you better interest rates than current accounts).

If you really want to grow your money, you're sorted. You know you've got all kinds of options. They might win contests for the most boring and technical-sounding things in the whole entire world *(stocks, bonds, certificates of deposit … I mean, really. Who names these things?!)* but they're good to know about. There are other, funkier things you can invest in too, like art and gold and cryptocurrencies, and you can do it yourself or invest through funds. But remember Warren Buffett – you need to know your stuff!

Finally, you know how to give your money. You know that the more wealth you have, the more money you can give. Because money gets a super bad reputation, but it can do some serious good in the world. It depends on what we decide to do with it. And even if we don't have money to give, we can always give our *time*, because that matters too.

So. Now you know all this, go out into this **AMAZING** world and **ENJOY IT.** Make money, make lots of it. **SPEND IT** the way you like. **SAVE IT** for a rainy day. Save it for a *hurricane*, though I hope you'll never encounter one. **GROW IT.** Sprinkle it into investments you really believe in and watch it grow thanks to our superhero friend, the power of compound interest. Build that wealth. Build and live the kind of life you've always dreamed of. And give. **GIVE GENEROUSLY.** Start small – wherever you're comfortable – but maybe one day you'll be a big giver. I hope you will. I believe you can be. *(Is that too cheesy for you? I thought I told you a bit of cheese never hurt anybody.)* OK, look, I get it. All that sounds so far into the future, doesn't it? Let's get back to **TODAY.** Today, it's the little things you do that'll make a difference. Things like buying from the good guys, giving away your pennies, and giving away your *time* wherever you can.

MONEY GETS A BAD REP. A REALLY BAD REP. LET'S GIVE IT A BETTER ONE. STARTING RIGHT NOW . . .